Hand to Mouth

ISBN 0-9543247 06

Acknowledgments: A restaurant is only as good as it's suppliers. Thanks, heartfelt indeed to:
A & S Baynes, Artesanía Alvarez, Barnitts, Conchifrit, Country Products, Cross of York,
David Swain, Exchange Coffee, Happy Hens, Los Hermanos Pedraza, Michael Lee,
Mike Rennison, Motaoliva, Silver Wolf, Spring Fine Foods, Symryn Sisters, Taste of Italy,
Via Vecchia, Vermex, Wards of York, York Catering Supplies.
Thanks also to Paul, Steve and crew who haul the rubbish with a smile, whatever the
weather...And last but by no means least Lawrence Holmes and Mark Withington, so expert at
improving and repairing our kitchen having done so, bless them, many times....
We have been helped so much on the creative side by Sian, Dave, Ken and Rob of Reprotech -
hard to imagine how the images would have ever translated so well without them... Writing a
book is as much an economic activity as a creative one, so finally we thank Jenny Noll,
Chris and Derek Utley, Lynne Vinicombe and the many patient creditors of El Piano

First published September 2002
Copyright ©ENDpapers
Images © ENDpapers

Distributed and published by
ENDpapers, P.O.Box 69, YORK, YO1 7WZ, England
Tel: +44 (0)1904 610676
Fax:+44 (0)1904 643049
Email: info @ ENDpapers.co.uk

Colour reproduction by Reprotech Studios, York

Printed by Studio Print, Guisborough

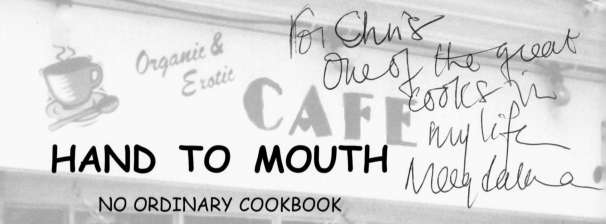

HAND TO MOUTH

NO ORDINARY COOKBOOK

Magdalena Chávez
Lisa Sharman
Rachel Stainsby

FOREWORD
Hugh Bayley MP

Photos thanks to
Andrew Dunn
Anna Harland
Alfredo Millett-Sikking
Rachel Stainsby
Polly Webb
with special thanks to
Ryszard Szydlo

Spanish and English language consultant
Candelaria García del Pino

FOREWORD

Two years ago I achieved a personal first by cooking in public as part of the York Festival of Food and Drink. It was in fact a double first because I also learned how to make a Spanish omelette. The facilitators of this remarkable event were the Hand to Mouth team and their aim was to illustrate how easy it can be to make nutritious meals for one. And it worked – I still use the recipe when I am away from home at the Houses of Parliament.

Writing for a cookbook is not something I've done before either, and it's as well that I'm contributing the FOREWORD rather than recipes. I have left that to the book's authors, each of whom has brought her own tastes, experiences and knowledge to their kitchen. When we are fortunate enough to have enough to eat and a choice as well, it seems right that we should take pleasure in our food. This cookbook shows the pleasure its authors take in creating and eating food and they are sharing that – rather like friends might share a meal.

As a survival cook myself, I am greatly encouraged by the lack of pictures in this book: there are no impossible assemblies of food to aspire to and never quite manage. Instead, Hand to Mouth offers a good read and a good feed.

Hugh Bayley

MP for City of York

September 2002

CONTENTS

CONTENTS

CONTENTS

INTRODUCCIÓN

Descubrir los colores de la naturaleza en la paleta del pintor y lograr con sus tonalidades un collage de comidas que luzca hermoso, cuyo sabor sea excelente y que al mismo tiempo alimente cuerpo y alma, es un arte ¿no es cierto? Y si bien es una habilidad el hacerlo rápidamente, es sobre todo una vocación el hacerlo cotidianamente, y para gente extraña.

Después de todo, la principal misión del cocinero es encontrar los ingredientes ocultos en ese delicioso sandwich, en ese souflé magistral, o en esa salsa oriental sin igual que se comió en aquella fiesta, en una cena, o en tal o cual restaurante...Para muchos cocineros, los platos que preparan son un ritual que en algún momento observaron y aprendieron de un familiar, de un amigo, o de un amante.

Porque quizás, cocinar sea una de las últimas tradiciones que se pasa de generación en generación, de mano en mano, de boca en boca; intentar volcar en papel toda esa tradición oral sin interponer una barrera de letras a ese río de conocimiento resulta ser todo un desafío.

Porque no hay palabras que puedan expresar la fragancia del agua de rosas, el color del azafrán, la elasticidad de la masa del pan, la suave tibieza del fruto maduro.

Porque tampoco hay palabras que puedan interceptar el instante en que una quiche esta a punto, a punto para el cocinero, o en el que la medida de sal es justa, justa para el comensal, o en que la mezcla es perfecta, perfecta para la fiesta.

Sólo en ese momento en que pasa del cocinero al consumidor se puede juzgar el éxito de la preparación: cuando se come, cuando reune gente, cuando se comparte, cuando es el puente entre el festejo y la danza; y cuando lo hace con delicadeza, con distinción, y sin embargo con vigor. Y cuando se terminó, se acabó.

Tampoco puede un cocinero decir: "ésta es mi receta". El cocinero es el punto de intersección de un número infinito de círculos que se entrecruzan. Su arte está formada por muchas manos anónimas que agregan su pizca de sal al plato final. Su libro de cocina de cabecera es en realidad, la influencia de centenares de personas que dieron forma a su repertorio con ejemplos y consejos. Un cocinero nunca está solo, trabaja codo a codo con un grupo de personas cercanas a él cuyo regalo nunca termina...

La gente que come en "El Piano" pregunta seguido "¿qué es esto? o ¿cómo haces esto otro?
En cambio, la gente que trabaja en "El Piano" me pregunta ¿dónde aprendiste esto? o ¿de dónde salió todo esto?

Quizás este libro rinde honor ambos.

Quizás este libro rinde honor a aquellos cocineros distinguidos que, a través de "El Piano", continuan aportando su granito de arena al collage de nuestra cocina.

Magdalena Sikking Chávez
Jefe de cocina y a veces, lavaplatos.
El Piano, YORK INGLATERRA

INTRODUCTION

It is an art, is it not, to work through the kaleidoscope of nature's colours and present a collage of food which looks beautiful, tastes excellent and nourishes body and soul? And while it is a skill to do so speedily, surely it is a vocation to do so daily, and for strangers.

The cook, afterall, is often recreating what he or she thinks might have been the contents of that delicious sandwich, that divine soufflé, this incomparable oriental sauce, eaten at that party, or the other dinner or in such and such a restaurant... At the same time the cook practises rituals observed and taught by the hands of friends, lovers, family. For cooking may be the last great tradition that is almost always passed, in some cases quite literally, from hand to mouth, mouth to hand, generation upon generation.

So it is a curiosity indeed to try to commit such an oral and manual tradition to paper, to interrupt as it were, a great flow of knowledge, with the cudgel of literacy. For no amount of words can accurately convey the scent of rose-water, the hue of tumeric, the elasticity of bread dough, the sweet warmth of over-ripe fruit.

Nor can words reliably intercept the moment when the quiche is baked right, right for the cook, or the salt is in correct measure, correct for the eater, or the mix is perfect, perfect for the party. Only at that point when it passes from the cook to its consumer can it be judged a success: when it is eaten; when it brings people together; when it is shared; when it forms the bridge upon which celebration is danced; when it does this deed delicately, distinctively yet with vigour.
And when it is done, it is gone.

Nor can any cook ever truly say, 'this is my recipe'. The cook's internal cookbook is in fact the influences of hundreds of people met over years who have shaped and moulded their repertoire with example and advice. A cook never stands alone but is always shoulder to shoulder with a distinguished group of his or her own private acquaintance, whose anonymous gifts continue through his or her hands.

People who eat at El Piano often say, 'what is this?' or 'how do you make this?'. In contrast, people who work at El Piano say 'where did you learn this?' or 'where did all this cooking come from?'

Perhaps this book does honour to both sets of enquiry and their enquirers.

Perhaps this book does honour to those distinguished but anonymous cooks who, through El Piano, continue to give their gifts.

Magdalena Sikking Chávez
Chief cook and sometime dishwasher
El Piano, YORK, ENGLAND

After he ran away to join the circus and before he drifted into riding freight trains, Roberto went north and drove cattle from California, across New Mexico and Arizona and sometimes as far as the stockyards in Kansas City. He said this was only as recently as the 1930s, about the time they brought electricity to San Bernardino and everyone was afraid no more children would be born because people would never go to bed if it was always light.

All the *vaqueros* will tell anyone that a tin jug is the only way to make coffee. In their world where every hour on the hoof today is directly equal to less flesh on the bone tomorrow, the cowboy, waiting for the coffee grounds to fall, in their own time, is himself released. He can ignore the relentless clock of sunup and sundown which measures the distance between the live weight and dead weight of the beasts at market.

Roberto said brewing coffee in a jug was a little bit of timeless heaven every day. He said tin jugs survive where pot and glass never would. He said, sieves, plungers, filters all take space, need washing when water is scarce. He said days were always too short, coffee made them a little longer, and convenience in food preparation has always been a factor...

Keep coffee, whether beans or ground, in the freezer (if not riding the range) use as needed – it keeps its flavour better ——

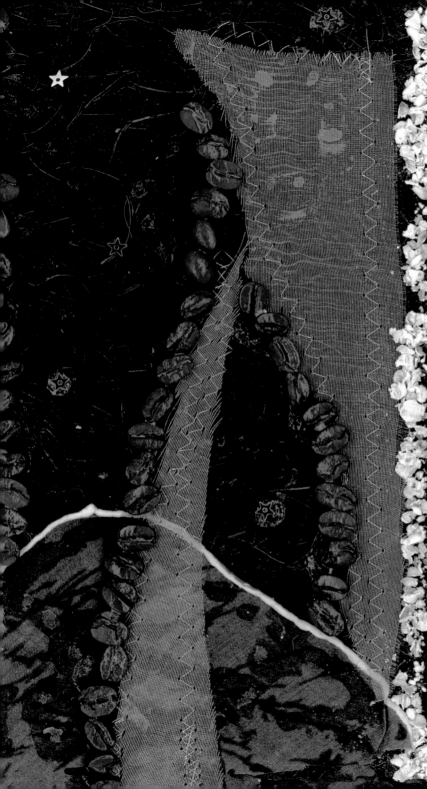

CHOCOLATE & MARSHMALLOW PIE

Make a wheat free base with 4 teacups of **oats**, 1 teacup each of melted **margarine** and **sugar** and a pinch of **salt**. Press into a pie dish. Cook 4 Tbl **cocoa** powder with ¾ litre of **soya milk**, pinch of **salt**, 1 teacup of **sugar** and 4 Tbl **cornflour**. Stir constantly until thick. Remove from heat and add two capfuls of **vanilla**. Fold in 20 **marshmallows**. They usually contain gelatine but vegan varieties can be found. Alternatively use **fruit chews**, **orange rind** or **toffees** to create interest. Pour into oatbase and cool.

COFFEE

It is fitting that on the first page a recipe for coffee should appear since the cookery reputation of the writers was built on the quality of the coffee they have served. Grind 2 heaped Tbl per person of **coffee beans**. Put the ground coffee in a warmed jug and immediately throw on boiling water. Wait. Wait some more. Stir. Wait again. When the grounds sink, sieve and serve. The coffee will be rich and strong but never bitter and there will be a thick creamy froth on the first cup poured.

Don Manuél holds olives in his hands as though they are pearls. In his factory in Granada they bring the harvest. Olives arrive amidst twigs and stones where they have been beaten from the trees with sticks so that the fruit falls on rough blankets to the earth below. Here the olives are graded, cleaned, stoned, or their faces cut ready for soaking in brine with herbs and fruits. On a low stool in rubber boots his wife can often be found shelling garlic or chunking lemons to add to the barrels. These two have been at work with olives since the time of Franco when no entrepreneur was welcome. Somehow they survived those years and now with sons, several thousand square feet of factory, mountains of pallets and employees joining them hard at work they still live with olives, many the size of plums, all glistening in their processes, fat with the promise of the taste of sunshine.

Overcook rice to make it sticky — rinse in water if overcooked by mistake — the grains will then separate.

OLIVES

Black **olives** have a sheen like gemstones and draw the eye of the eater to them as the focal point for any garnish. Use them in potato salad or pasta sauce for contrast, smash them up in olive oil for tapanade, keep them in olive oil until the oil takes their flavour and they are bland enough for breakfast. Rejoice in the picual that delivers such a peppery oil…

SUSHI

Using **nori** sheets prepare sushi, or Japanese starters, by toasting the seaweed sheets until they take on a luminous green sheen. Remove and lay on a bamboo rolling sheet. Press onto the nori about ½ centimetre of cooked **rice**. Sushi rice is easier to handle because it sticks together but in fact any rice will do. Add a tiny layer first of grated **carrots** and then **spring onions**. Include fresh or pickled **ginger** if desired, **wasabi** paste or a dash of **shoyu** or **tamari**. Use the bamboo sheet as a tool to roll up the nori more easily into a long sausage shape. Leave to rest. Then cut in slices. The green spring onions form the centre, then a ring of orange carrot, then white rice, finally black nori. Serve cold.

brown

BROWN

brown

A
African Groundnut Stew
Apple Fritters

B
Brownies
Carrot Cake

C
Coffee & Bailey's Cheese Cake
Nut Loaf
Patatas a lo Pobre

P
Peanut Sauce
Pinchitos

S
Samosas
Thai Mince
Topside of Beef

The woman who came to the bakery was a regular. And she was rich. One of those customers who orders and never asks the price: puts it all in the basket, hands over the money, never counts the change. She'd lived for a while in Africa. Botswana to be precise. She talked, not of the poverty, nor the swollen stomachs, not a word about corruption, broken promises or fading hopes. She talked of the simple foods, the delicacy of the cuisine, the gentle but clear-cut flavours. She talked of sunsets, of the scent of Africa, of the wildlife, of what seemed on first listening to be the observations of the privileged. It wasn't that she never knew the other, it's just she chose not to dignify it through idle conversation. ✫ ★ ★ ✩

Less can be more...thin flavousome stews drizzled over rice are as good as thick & chunky ones...

AFRICAN GROUND NUT STEW

Dice very finely 1 green or red **pepper**, 1 **leek** and fry them in 2 Tbl **vegetable oil**. Add 4 oz, ½ cup of coarsely chopped redskin **peanuts**, or any other peanut which is not roasted nor salted and 6 skinned **tomatoes** or, alternatively 3 Tbl tomato paste. Fry a bit longer. Then add 2 heaped tsp **tumeric**, 3 tsp **cumin seeds**, pinch of **salt** and 3 cups of water. Simmer gently for a long time, the longer the better, as much as 5 hours…although it is perfectly edible after 30 mins. It should be thin and watery and served over **rice**. ✶

Perfect basmati rice is achieved by these simple steps.
- ➤ Boil twice the quantity of water to rice.
- ➤ Once the water is boiling throw in the rice.
- ➤ Stir.
- ➤ Wait until the water comes back to the boil, stir again.
- ➤ Reduce heat to half or less, put on the lid and don't look for 20 minutes.
- ➤ Serve hot or rinse and serve cold.

Perfect.

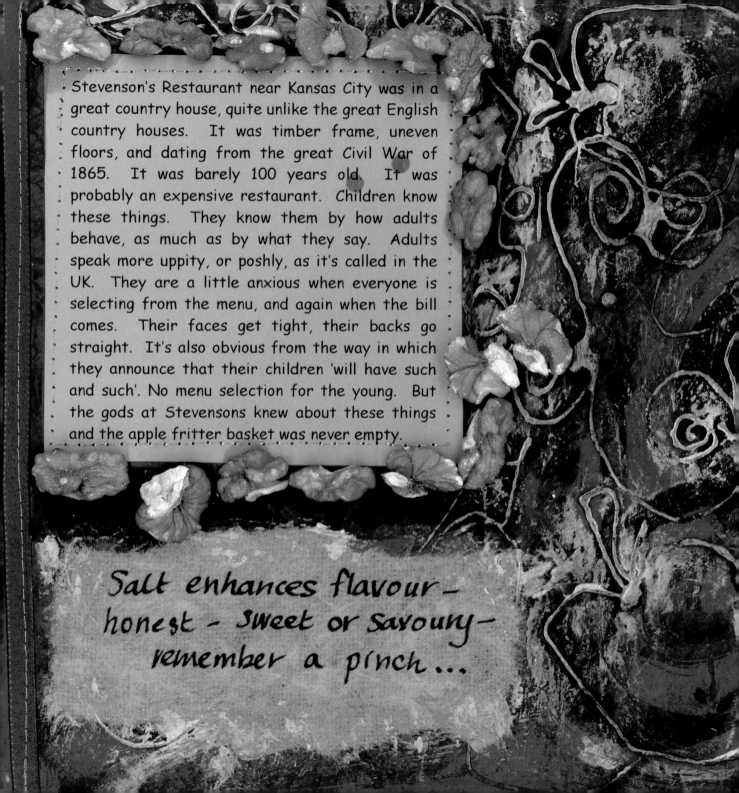

Stevenson's Restaurant near Kansas City was in a great country house, quite unlike the great English country houses. It was timber frame, uneven floors, and dating from the great Civil War of 1865. It was barely 100 years old. It was probably an expensive restaurant. Children know these things. They know them by how adults behave, as much as by what they say. Adults speak more uppity, or poshly, as it's called in the UK. They are a little anxious when everyone is selecting from the menu, and again when the bill comes. Their faces get tight, their backs go straight. It's also obvious from the way in which they announce that their children 'will have such and such'. No menu selection for the young. But the gods at Stevensons knew about these things and the apple fritter basket was never empty.

Salt enhances flavour - honest - sweet or savoury - remember a pinch ...

APPLE FRITTERS

Per person served, grate 1 **cooking apple**, 1 tsp **butter** or **margarin**e, ½ cup water or **milk** and enough self-raising **flour** to form marble sized balls. Deep fry in **sunflower oil**, drain and roll in **icing sugar** and **cinnamon**. Best served hot.

BROWNIES

Whizz together 1 cup **cocoa**, 500g tub melted **margarine**, using the same tub for 1 tub each **sugar** and **soya milk** and up to 2 of self raising **flour** to make a thick batter. Add 2 capsful of **vanilla** and a good pinch of **salt**. If you leave out the salt they will be tasteless like powder, promise! Pour into a greased floured oven sized baking tray and bake slowly until set but moist in the middle. Cool, cut and serve. A **walnut** piece in the middle of each square is ideal.

So, what's
your story?

CARROT CAKE

Mix together 4 cups each of grated **carrots**, **self-raising flour** with 2 cups each **sunflower oil**, **sugar**, and 1 each of **raisins** and **walnuts**. Add 1 heaped tsp **cinnamon**, and the zest and juice of 1 **orange**. Bake in a cake pan in a medium oven, about an hour, or until a knife comes out clean.

COFFEE AND BAILEY'S CHEESECAKE

Make a wheat-free base with 4 teacups of **oats**, 1 teacup each of melted **margarine** and **sugar** and a pinch of **salt**. Flavour the base with 1 Tbl Bailey's liqueur. Mix 4 **eggs** with 3 teacups of **cream cheese**, 1 teacup each of milk and sugar, 3 Tbl Baileys, 1 tsp instant coffee and a teaspoon of **vanilla**. Pour into the pie dish and bake in a low to medium oven for an hour. The slower the bake the more even the colour…

When Little Bob was three, Franco had been dead more than twenty years. On one of those long night hauls up from Granada to Bilbao, with the payload at the limit, and that blue darkness that makes a highway stretch out into a peaceful and anonymous forever, his little voice piped up from the shadows.

"Let's chat Mamá," he said.

"What about?"

"Let's chat about Franco..."

An odd topic for one so young...

"Why Franco?"

"Well, Pepe's grandma says that we should eat our patatas a lo pobre. They are rich she says, olive oil is our gold. She says in the time of Franco that was all they had."

Take care when substituting wheat flour with rice flour – it swells hugely – and, remember lentils have great setting qualities when cold.

NUT LOAF

Just to confuse matters, this nut roast doesn't have to be made of nuts. Baked in a loaf pan, it is designed to be turned out, sliced and served, hot with gravy or cold with chutneys. Use 1 cup each of **nuts**, diced **onions**, sieved **tomatoes**, 3 **eggs**, 1 Tbl mixed **herbs**, 1 tsp **salt**. Add **breadcrumbs** or oats to bind to dough-like consistency. Press into the loaf pan and bake 1 hour in a medium oven. Or, ditch the nuts and go for 2 cups cooked red or green **lentils**, no eggs, 1 cup of diced onions, 1 Tbl mixed herbs, 1 tsp salt, and oats or breadcrumbs to bind to a dough-like consistency and bake as above. For gluten free, substitute gram, potato, or rice flour for oats or breadcrumbs.

PATATAS A LO POBRE

Slice each two good-sized **potatoes** and ½ **onion** per person and **salt**. Leave 20 minutes until the water has seeped out of the potatoes. Fry in a bath of **olive oil** until the potatoes break up. Drain and serve. Red or green **peppers** are an optional extra. Simple but delicious.

When the restaurant was new a little Thai woman came in looking for work with hardly any words other than Thai. She presented several covered pots.

There were some coconut and peanut sauces with lemon grass and lime leaves, several dark savoury sweetmeats and light fluffy dumplings. A peanut concoction and a fish paste rarity...

The edible resumé was sampled and smiles were exchanged. A date to begin was agreed. She went and never came back.

But the taste of that CV never left...

Pineapple juice is an awesome tenderizer the acid breaks fibres down fast - a great marinade for tough (cheap) cuts of meat...

PEANUT SAUCE

A dressing for salads, or a sauce for stir-fry, this requires a host of ingredients. Blend 1 Tbl each **peanut butter** and sweet **sherry**. Add a tsp each of grated **ginger** and **garlic** coated in **sunflower oil**. Add a bunch of finely chopped **spring onions**, 1 tsp **sugar**, pinch of **salt**, **soya sauce** or **tamari**. Stop here. For salad dressing, add **rice vinegar** to taste. For stir fry add **coconut milk** to the pint mark and pour over any stir fried vegetables. The sauce will thicken when heated as coconut milk is a natural thickener.

PINCHITOS

It's all in the marinade. Use a kilo of cubed **pork** for about 8 people, although they wish more had been done…Marinade for 4 hours at least in dash each of **olive oil** and **white wine**, one sliced **onion** and 1 tsp of **turmeric**, **paprika**, **cumin**, **salt**, **ground coriander** and **pepper**. Either flash fry until cooked or skewer and bar-b-q or griddle.

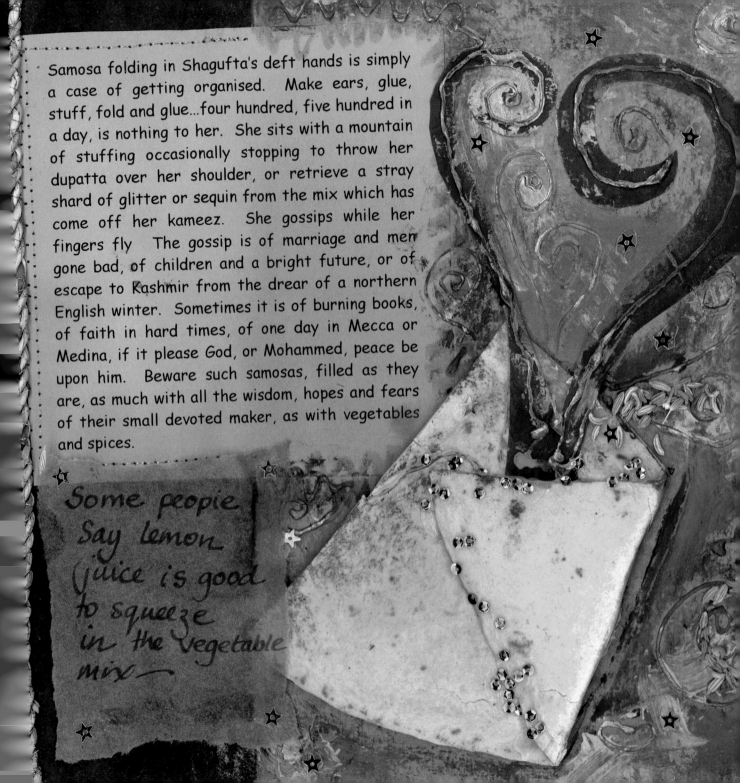

Samosa folding in Shagufta's deft hands is simply a case of getting organised. Make ears, glue, stuff, fold and glue...four hundred, five hundred in a day, is nothing to her. She sits with a mountain of stuffing occasionally stopping to throw her dupatta over her shoulder, or retrieve a stray shard of glitter or sequin from the mix which has come off her kameez. She gossips while her fingers fly The gossip is of marriage and men gone bad, of children and a bright future, or of escape to Kashmir from the drear of a northern English winter. Sometimes it is of burning books, of faith in hard times, of one day in Mecca or Medina, if it please God, or Mohammed, peace be upon him. Beware such samosas, filled as they are, as much with all the wisdom, hopes and fears of their small devoted maker, as with vegetables and spices.

Some people say lemon juice is good to squeeze in the vegetable mix—

SAMOSAS

Triangular deep fried parcels, these are a winner hot or cold. Use **flour tortillas** for the 'skins', cut them into four, and fold them according to the illustration. Stuff them with a mix of 2K **potatoes**, 1K **carrots** diced and boiled until soft. Before draining add 1 large diced **onion** and either 1 cup frozen **peas** or a similar amount of diced **broccoli**. The hot water will soften these two but their colour and flavour will be retained. Drain.

Now the spices: 2 Tbl each of **cumin seeds, fennel seeds** and **Madras curry powder**. 1 heaped tsp **salt**. Add a huge bunch of chopped **fresh coriander**.

Mix and prepare to stuff. Create a 'glue' of **flour** and water, fold the samosa 'skins' as illustrated and 'glue' the seams. Either deep fry in **sunflower oil** until golden brown or freeze and fry at a later date. Makes 130.

Serve with **raita** (see WHITE section, or mint sauce of **yoghurt**, fresh or bottled **mint**, **sugar**, **vinegar** and a dash of **chilli** if desired.

27

Food at the *Tia Abuela's* (great aunt's) was always good, mostly because there was plenty. Meanness of spirit always shows through a cook's hand...when meat is scarce, the thickness of the slice tells the largness of the carver's heart...when the bean crop has failed the presence of last year's bottled lentils tells the guest the value of their visit. When time is short the timing of the marinade and the slowness of the roast speak volumes for the forethought.

Lemon grass and lime leaves are a good addition to any Thai style meal — but, just like bay leaves, DON'T EAT THEM

THAI MINCE

Fry 2 diced **onions** in a wok until golden brown with sufficient **sunflower oil** to cover them generously. Add a pint measure of **soya mince** (TVP) and let the mince soak up the oil but ensure that it doesn't scorch. Add a whole tin of **hoi sin** sauce (8oz) and a good pint of water, more as necessary as the mince soaks up the liquid. Salt to taste. Finally fold in one chopped fresh **pineapple** and a bunch of chopped fresh **coriander** leaves. Either fold into samosas (see this BROWN section), or serve over rice.

TOPSIDE OF BEEF

Make sure to get organic **beef** with fat on it. Marinade it in **garlic, peppercorns, onions, salt pepper** and **red wine**. Leave in the marinade and gently roast, 20 minutes to the pound, in a covered dish. For the final 10 mins blast the heat to brown off the fat. Remove and let it rest before carving. If served cold, weight it so as to slice it easily. (see PINK section).

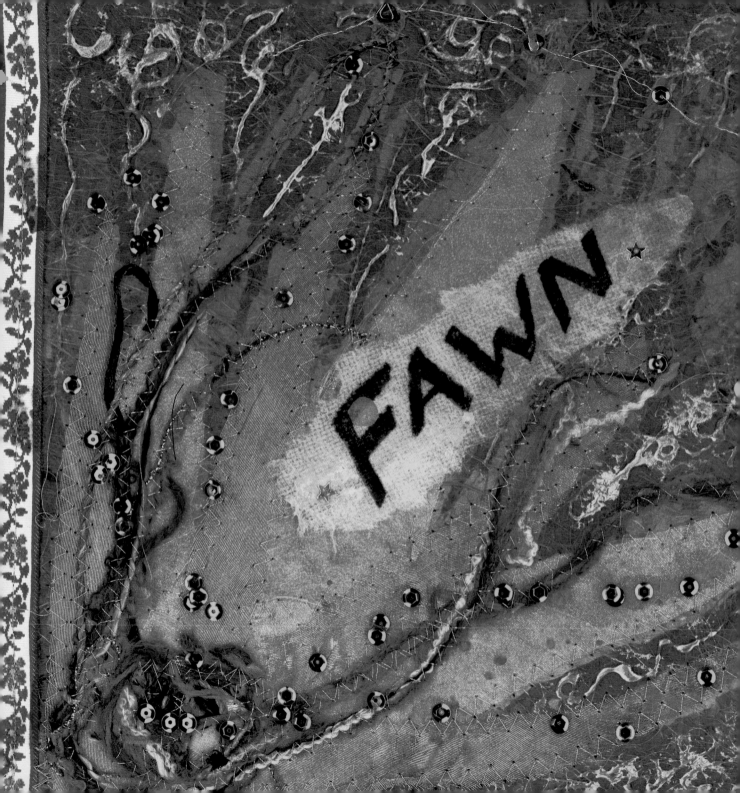

Aubergine Pâté

Roast Pork

Pacific Poké

Sweet Creams

In the West Riding of Yorkshire, not that long ago, children wore wooden clogs and lived many to a room in back to back housing. The buildings were tall, narrow and dark and gardenless. Some say it was like living in lift shafts. And the men and women worked long hours in the weaving sheds and went deaf to the clatter of the looms.

The women took the weekly joint to the bakers, since cellar-top kitchens rarely sported an oven sufficient to the task. Vera was a great fan of pork, cheap, juicy and, best of all, filling. The fat could be spread on bread, the juices reserved for soup and there was never any waste. Vera is well past eighty now, still living in her 'lift shaft'. She says she can still see in her mind's eye the children resonating down the cobbles kicking up sparks from the clog irons. She still likes pork, which she can now roast in her own oven...

Tofu or cream cheese are great bases to build pâtes on: be creative... mushrooms, basil and sherry; chestnuts; cranberries & juniper...

AUBERGINE PÂTÉ

The delicate flavour of aubergines needs careful handling if it is not to be lost in making pâté. Roast 4 **aubergines** in the oven until the skins are like paper, scrape out the middles and whizz with 1 tsp **cumin seeds**, pinch **salt** and enough **orange juice** to make the consistency required for either dip or pâté. Adjust the salt as needed. Leave, ideally overnight, for the flavours to mingle.

ROAST PORK

Choose an organic **pork** joint with plenty of fat on the outside, get rolled shoulder if possible, it is sweeter and has more flavour. Organic pork is almost always more flavourful anyway. Score the fat in rows. Roast in a medium oven a good 20 minutes to the pound and ideally uncovered. A fatty joint needs less protection from shrinkage. Half an hour before the end, rub **salt** and **hot mustard powder** into the scored fat. Whack up the heat. Presto, crackling. Remove, allow to rest 5 minutes and serve.

33

Astrid brought a book of street food to show the variety of portable delicacies across the world. As well as recipes the book was stuffed full of photos of people selling, eating, preparing great fistfuls of every conceivable food from salads, to curries, to noodles, to, yep, POKÉ. The recipe here has moved the recipe there along, adding some of this and some of that. Now, instead of something for the mouth delivered by a hand it's mode of transport is a plate and a fork. The version here is trumped up to some extent, its humble origins laced over with a base and a pie shape to accommodate cutlery and crockery rather than a hand. But the part for the mouth is just as good...

Sweet toppings are easy when you know the principles: tofu, bananas, ground nuts are all a great base to build on...

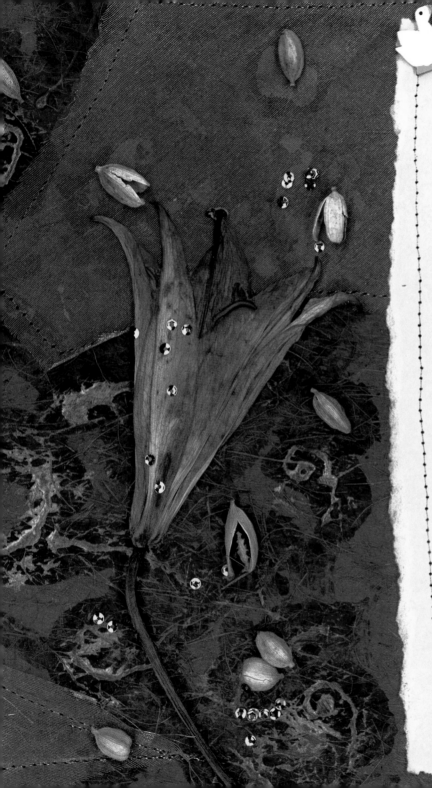

PACIFIC POKE

Make a wheat free base with 4 teacups of **oats**, 1 teacup each of melted **margarine** and **sugar** and a pinch of **salt**. Whizz together six bananas, pinch each of salt and ground cinnamon, 2-3 Tbl brown sugar, a block of creamed coconut and boiling water up to a pint, or pint and ½. Pour over the base and bake in a slow oven for 40 mins or until the pie is solid. Serve warm or cold.

SWEET CREAMS

➢ Whizz tofu with sugar, orange juice and orange zest…
➢ Cook rice flour (1 measure rice flour to 6 of liquid) with water or soya milk, cocoa powder, pinch of salt and vanilla to taste…
➢ Grind cashews or almonds, whizz up with water or soya milk, green cardemoms, seeds, sugar and vanilla…
➢ Blend brandy with vanilla and sugar and soya milk, thicken by heating gently with cornflour…
➢ Use coconut milk with pineapple or cinnamon, thicken with cornflour or by whizzing with a banana…

Cashew burgers
Felafels
Flapjax
Tabouleh

Florine was keen on the French style. She went to a Swiss finishing school and learned cordon blue. Sauces, creams, sherries and Madeiras were very much her metier. She married an all American boy, did the career thing and kept a good all American home. The thing was though, she was a good Jewish girl, and despite all her skill in haute cuisine, she loved a good felafel. And, my good ness, she could make one. See, you can take the girl out of the traditonal kitchen, but you can't take the traditional kitchen out of the girl...

Don't add too many oats, they soak up moisture or, knowing they do, use them to correct too much liquid

CASHEW BURGERS

Pulverise 1 Tbl **cashews** per person served. Add the same of **oats**, **gram** (chick pea) **flour** and water. A pinch of **salt** and **marjoram** bring out the flavour. Adjust water and oats so mix holds together while shallow fried in **sunflower oil**.

FELAFELS

Use 3 pints cooked **chick peas**, 2 finely chopped **onions**, 2 tsp. **garlic**, **lemon juice**, 1 tsp each **salt**, **ground cumin** and **coriander**. Liquidise or mash until smooth, but allow some texture. Add finely chopped **parsley**. Consistency is important: moist enough to form into balls, solid enough to hold its shape. Add either water or **gram** (chick pea) **flour**. Form into ping pong sized balls, coat in gram flour. Fry just one in **sunflower oil**. Adjust seasonings. Fry them all. Makes loads. Freezes well. Serve with…

…FIRE SAUCE

Liquidise 2 fresh **chillis** and 2 **onions** in plenty of **olive oil** Fry until soft. Add pinch of **salt**, 2 Tbl of **tomato purée**, and scant water to make a thick sauce. Boil rapidly until reduced. Ready.

Nothing grows in the archipelago of Los Roques except fish. 30 minutes by plane from Caracas, Venezuela, the food boat comes on Thursdays and is followed by Bedlam. The islanders fight their way to the promise of sea weary limp vegetables and fruit.

Parsley stands no chance in the belly of a boat. But Marie Eugenia flew in one morning with a bunch of fresh green healthy juicy parsley under her arm and nothing else. She put it all into the tabouleh...sheer luxury. Not a grain was uneaten.

Don't overwork the flapjax mix - it will go claggy and clumpy... less is more...

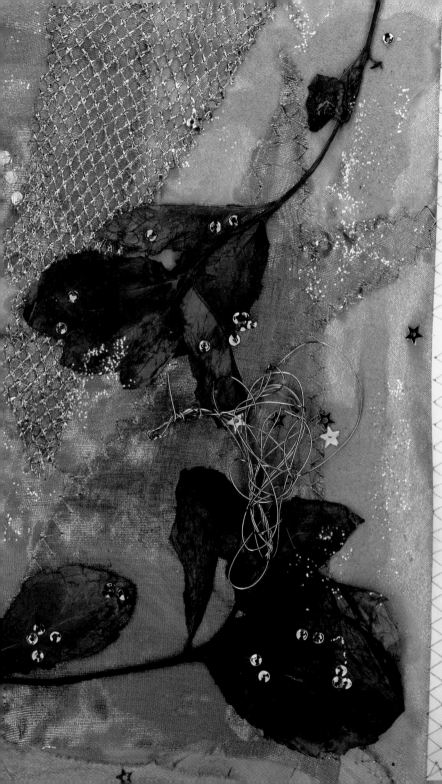

FLAPJAX

Melt 500g of **margarine** and pour onto 1K **porridge oats**. Add 500g **brown sugar**, a pinch of **salt** and hand mix. Press half the mix into an oven proof dish. Layer on a pint of cooked sour **apples** with **cinnamon** and **raisins**, or ¾ pint of **dates** or **apricots** softened in hot water and whizzed with a bit of **orange peel**. Whatever pleases. Layer on the rest of the oat mix. Press down and bake at medium to gentle heat for 20 – 30 minutes. Cut while warm, remove when cold. 16 massive flapjax.

TABOULEH

Wash and soak **bulgar wheat** in warm water until very slightly chewy. Drain. Add pinch of **salt** to six diced **tomatoes**, half a **cucumber** and some **spring onions**. Finely chop a big handful of **fresh parsley** and a smaller amount of **mint**. Dried mint will do but the parsley must be fresh. Mix altogether with the juice of a **lemon** and enough **olive oil** to coat each grain. Allow to stand for flavours to mingle and the wheat to finish swelling in the juices. Adjust salt or liquid as needed.

- Celery Salad
- Lentil Dhal
- Jade Salad
- Olives
- Puy Lentils
- Spinach & Pine Nut Quiche
- Stilton Parcels
- Stuffed Chillis
- Stuffed Vine Leaves

Imagine the delight of an Hispanic refugee in a northern European country finding a cookbook on Asian food written by someone with a name like Jack Santa Maria. He wrote a lentil dhal recipe using coconut milk which inspired this. How Jack Santa Maria came to be writing an Asian cookery book remains a mystery, but the beauty of his dhal, transfigured herewith, marches on.

DON'T salt pulses until the END — it retards the cooking process

Pure Creamed Coconut

coriander

CELERY SALAD

A great solution for a celery mountain this salad is four parts diced **celery**, one part diced green eating **apple**, 1 part diced **cucumber** and 1 part **pumpkin seeds**. Simply mix and serve.

LENTIL DHAL

The title in fact means 'lentil lentil' since dhal is lentil in Hindi but this is the English version.... Fry the holy trinity of 1 **onion**, tsp grated fresh **ginger** and a tsp grated fresh **garlic** in sunflower **oil**. When soft add 2 tsps of Madras **curry powder** and a good sized teacup of split **red lentils**. Fry the curry powder and the lentils in the oil until all the lentils are coated. Using the same tea-cup add three full of water and half a block of solid **cream coconut**. Coconut milk is better if available and simply use it to replace the water. Add more water if necessary as the lentils cook. Finally, when the lentils have mushed remove from the heat, **salt** to taste and add a good bunch of fresh chopped **coriander**.

Hugh Carpenter ran a cookery course which Roanne attended. Sheet upon sheet of oriental recipes of which his Jade Salad was one. She took the best of him and adapted it to her kitchen. In her case, more prawns, ...But like all good recipes, it was a guide, and remains volatile. Prawns are possible additions of course, as is chicken, pork, tofu cubes...sweet red ginger was an original intention replaced here with fresh ginger, equally, pine kernals will do instead of almonds. The point is this; cooking is both an art and a learned skill, humans are born knowing what tastes good, but not how to make it taste good. What Hugh taught he learned and adapted, what Roanne learned she adapted and then taught and so knowledge goes round...

after chopping—turn the knife and use the spine to scrape the chopped food from the board to its destination—it dulls the blade less.

JADE SALAD

The sharply contrasting colours and the dressing are what make this salad so orientally special. Toss together 4 parts fresh **spinach** with 1 part thinly sliced **red peppers**, one part diced **spring onions**, 1 part toasted **flaked almonds**. Dress with a mix of 6 Tbl **sunflower oil**, 2 Tbl **rice vinegar**, **1 tsp sugar**, zest and **juice** of one **orange**, tsp grated **fresh ginger**, dash of **soya sauce**. Simply mix and serve.

GREEN OLIVES

Olives are as varied as apples; fat, wrinkled, mild, sharp, fleshy. Similarly they have distinct flavours be they smoky, fruity, sunny, peppery, or briny. Use in salads, or serve alone or with bread. Use as garnish, stone and stuff with anchovies, roasted peppers, nuts, citrus peel. Even smash up and steep in olive oil before spreading thinly on toast…

Apart from running a sideline in fertility earrings, Rosara fancied herself a healer. Venezuelan dysentery is a pernicious beast, knowingly referred to by many a gringo as 'Montazuma's revenge'. She ladled out a watery green bean broth laced with garlic and doubtless magic words and set it before her weakened patients. The soup rarely eradicated the symptoms but the savoury aroma whetted the appetite and wakened the will to eat. Afterall half the battle on the road to healing is desire.

place your palm over the tortillas & pour the mix over your hand. It stops them floating

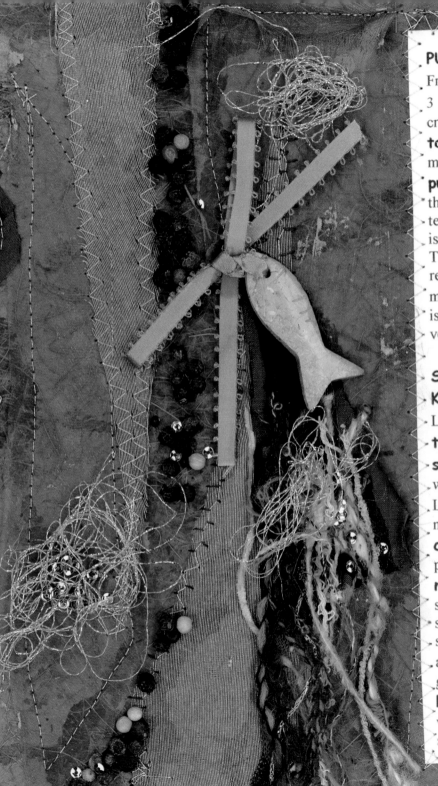

PUY CAVIAR

Fry 3 cloves of grated **garlic** in 3 Tbl **olive oil** until soft, not crisp. Add 2 liquidised fresh **tomatoes**. Cook gently 5 minutes. Add 2 cups of rinsed **puy lentils**. Let them absorb the flavours before adding 3 teacups water. Cook until water is absorbed, add more if needed. The lentils should be soft yet retain their shape, about 30 minutes. **Salt** to taste. There is nothing watery about this version, they are like caviar….

SPINACH & PINE KERNEL QUICHE

Line a flan dish with **flour tortillas**. Wash a bag of **spinach**, drain, then heat until wilted down. Drain again. Liquidise 6 **eggs** with a pint of milk, 1 heaped tablespoon of **cream cheese**, 1 **onion**, a pinch each of freshly grated **nutmeg** and **salt**. Add in the spinach and scarcely liquidise so as to keep small pieces for a speckled look. Pour into dish and sprinkle with **pine kernels** gently so they don't sink. Add **black pepper**. To retain the vibrant green colour, bake very slowly, until set.

49

Larry used to drive trucks between Los Angeles and San Francisco, stopping in San Jose most trips to change loads. Sometimes, north of Los Angeles if he felt chatty he would take on a hitch-hiker or two and occasionally, if things went well, he would offer them a return trip southward the following week. By such means regular acquaintance can establish.

Like many immigrants he worked long hours sending most of his money home to wife and family. He played little but when he did, he played hard. A night of Harvey Wallbanger's in Los Angeles led to a day of recovery on the long haul north. Chillies were a must for all who suffered. They give fire, ire and desire, said Larry.

In April 2002 at Robert & Louise's wedding in York, alongside a night of celebration and indulgence, fire, ire and desire were served up in a mountain of stuffed chillies. Thanks to Larry for that longer lasting acquaintance.

After preparing chillies take care with toileting, nose picking and rubbing eyes, it hurts!

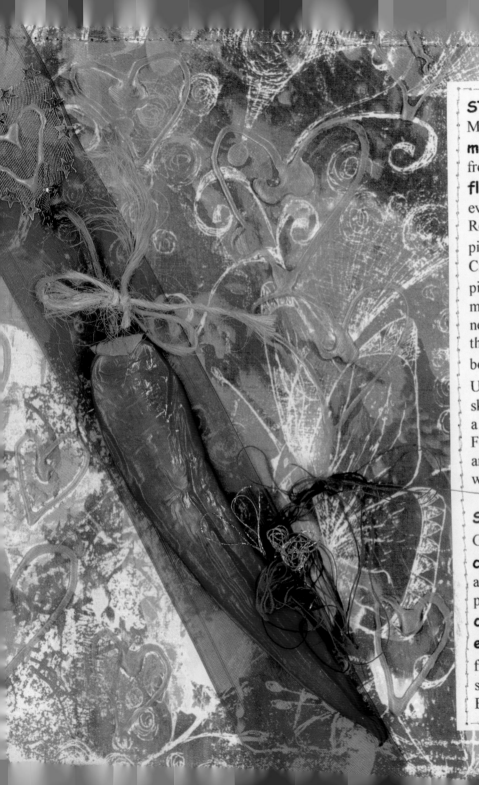

STILTON PARCELS

Make a sauce with 3 Tbl **margarine** or **butter**, remove from heat and stir in 3 Tbl plain **flour**, white or brown, so that every grain is coated in fat. Return to heat and slowly add a pint of **milk**, stirring constantly. Crumble in a good hand sized piece of **stilton**. If the cheese is mature no extra salt will be needed. Stir the sauce until thickened. Add in six large boiled and cubed **potatoes**. Using **tortilla wraps** as the skins place at the centre of each a generous tablespoon the mix. Fold the skins around the mix and bake in the over topping with any leftover sauce.

STUFFED CHILLIS

Get the fat stubby **green chillis** and take off their tops and core out as many seeds as possible. Stuff with a mix of **corn meal**, **onions**, **salt** and **egg** or water. Deep or shallow fry in **sunflower oil** until the skins brown and crack. Serve. Especially at weddings.

The boy made a coffee with so much sugar it was almost undrinkable, more like spoonable. The texture was of powder, so fine was the grind and so thick the nectar. He placed it on the engraved brass tray. Only the best of everything for the visitor. The sand stretched out to the Greek sea connecting his single story square dwelling to the beach front high rise hotel.

When the dolmades arrived, a simple stuffed vine leaf, their salt taste combined with the sea air, cut the thick sweetness of the coffee like a knife. They were perfect for each other.

STUFFED VINE LEAVES

Vine leaves are easy to find preserved in brine. First immerse them in water, not only to remove the preservative, but also to loosen the leaves which are delicate and become stuck together in the shrink packaging process. Then, leaf by leaf, separate them and stack them all the same way, the veins to the top, the smooth surface to the bottom. Prepare a stuffing of uncooked **rice** grains with a finely diced **onion** and the juice of a **lemon**. The leaves provide the salt. For a packet of leaves, making about 50, no more than a heaped teacup of rice is necessary. In the centre of each leaf put less than a tsp of the rice mix. Fold the leaves in as shown on this page. Place them all tenderly in a steamer. Feel free to stack them. Weight the stack in the steamer with a plate allowing water to extend into the steaming chamber. It is fine if some of the parcels are covered. Cook until the rice swells and is soft. Cool the parcels and serve cold with **mayo**, **tomato sauce**, **dill**, whatever…

Fridges are trying. Leaves you keep best a plastic bag insed in cold water.

53

Some people do with fabric what others do with food. Natalie replaced black and white with

sunshine yellow, deep cerise, ravishing red, noisy orange, opulent purple...and sometimes a little

indigo if the mood took her. With a smile as bright as the colours, her presence brightened

the lives of those around her and brought her smiles and more colours in return.

Kaleidescope

Everyone knows that angels wear white and have wings. Except for those that masquerade as rainbows and wear smiles.

Chopped
salad
Flour tortilla
tower
Roast vegeta
bles
Tofu garden
Tofu in sweet
& sour
sauce

The two of them worked nights, he tall dark and handsome, she voluptuous and willing. They exchanged life stories while peeling potatoes and breathing dreams over washing up. Too much Tequila and a twist of confidence took them from cooking up the standard recipes to cooking up something more. Emptying the fridge of leftover beans and sauces, finding a forgotten tub of cream cheese, discovering last night's sautéed mushrooms, they layered them between flour tortillas, colour by colour, until a tower resulted. A triumph.

Spread cream cheese & refried beans using a wet hand —

then it doesn't stick to you...

CHOPPED SALAD

Thanks to the anonymous chef at the Beach Country Club who only ever chops his salads by hand so as not to bruise the food, this is a salad of jewel-like beauty. Cut every piece the same size, go for contrasts, red **apples**, **peppers**, **broccoli**, purple and white **cabbages**, **seeds** and **nuts**, **cheeses**, **salamis**…use any dressing…

KALEIDESCOPE FLAN

Very fast, very easy, looks very impressive. Build a tower in a flan dish, layering **leftovers** between **flour tortillas**. Interleave **refried beans**, **cream cheese**, **pasta sauce**, sautéed **mushrooms**, puréed **greens**. Whatever, provided the colours contrast, it will look great. Leave overnight so that the tortillas absorb the leftovers' moisture and it all holds together. Turn out, easing if necessary with a knife. Slice like a flan, microwave or heat gently.

ROAST VEGETABLES

Peel and evenly chop **onions**, **potatoes**, **parsnips**, **sweet potatoes**, **peppers**… Go for colour contrasts. **Salt** and toss in **olive oil**, roast 45-60 mins.

Before Soo Lee gave over control of her restaurant to other cooks she made a vegetable stir fry that looked just like a flower garden: the green of the spinach shining, the onions translucent, the peppers like jewels against the deep dark dots of black bean. It had an iridescent depth, almost an insistence on being eaten. The sauce had the sweetness of the vegetables and sultry salted smoke of black beans. She used to laugh at the compliments, but she knew its pulling power and for a long time it was hard to persuade her to sell those little yellow drums of black beans to those who wanted to try and repeat her magic at home. In the end, she must have decided that magic is stronger for being shared, for she did.

Cooking spinach shrinks it big time. Best use raw & throw some hot food over it.

The leaves will wilt but retain some bulk & vitamins

TOFU GARDEN & SWEET & SOUR TOFU

Distinct dishes due to the sauce:

Black bean: Soak a handful of dried and usually smelly **black beans**. After 20 mins drain beans and set aside. Retain liquid and mix with 1 Tbl each **sugar**, **soya sauce** or **tamari** and **cornflour**.

Sweet and sour: Mix 1 Tbl each **tomato purée**, **sugar**, **vinegar** and **cornflour**. Add 4 Tbl water.

The rest is the same.

Wash a handful of chopped **spinach** or **spring greens**. Set aside. Chop for stir frying **onions**, **carrots**, **courgettes**, **peppers**, **mushrooms**, **corn**, **red cabbage**, whatever, go for contrasts. Chop all the same size. Set aside in separate groups. Plan on one whole vegetable feeding one person, ie eight different vegetables for eight servings etc. Choose 500g set **tofu**, cut into postage stamp sized cubes. Shallow fry in **sunflower oil** until golden. Drain and toss onto the spinach or greens. Fry grated **ginger** and **garlic** in the remaining oil. Add vegetables according to length of time they take to cook. Stir-fry. Finally add the chosen sauce, stir until thickened, pour over tofu and spinach and serve.

- Carrot & Coriander Soup

- Carrot Salad
    - Chick Pea Burgers
    - Chick Pea & Potato Curry

- Lasagna
- Sweet Potato Mousse

The children used to be drawn to carrots like insects are to yellow. Something in the colour and the sweetness made them play with carrots <u>and</u> eat them. Or so it was believed. Later, when time had put a distance between those early years and the sophistication of young adulthood, they were asked what had been the attraction to so simple a dish, thinking the reply would have a logic.

'the rabbits eat them and we wanted to be like them.'

'what? free to run? to be soft and furry?'

'oh no.' they said, 'to see the world clearly.'

Garnish soups with fresh leaves or grated cheese or cream or even just ground pepper or nutmeg or paprika — move from mundane to gourmet...

CARROT & CORIANDER SOUP

In **olive oil** fry, per person served, ½ an **onion** and 4 **carrots**. Use a Tbl of olive oil per person served and a thick bottomed pan as the frying needs to be lengthy so that the sweetness of the carrot and the onions is well extracted and both are brown, soft and breaking up. Only then add the water, 1 ½ cups per person. Cook until the carrots are fully cooked. Liquidise with fresh **coriander**, one good bunch per 4 people and **salt** to taste.

CARROT SALAD

Simply grated **carrots**. That's it. Dressed with **citrus juice** they stay orange longer. Add **poppy seeds** for contrast although it can make people look funny when the seeds are stuck between their teeth. **Raisins** are a common favourite addition, or grated **coconut**. The best thing about the salad is the bright colour it lends any dish and its popularity with children.

Chick pea burgers are very portable. Miranda made them with rice, deep fried them and wrapped them in newspaper. She ate them on and off for a full 24 hours from London to Provence. Outside Paris, not unlike Boule de Suife, she shared them with strangers, but unlike Boule de Suife, met no Prussians. She said garlic was always a good idea...

Always pre-cook potatoes for curries- otherwise they stay bullet-hard..

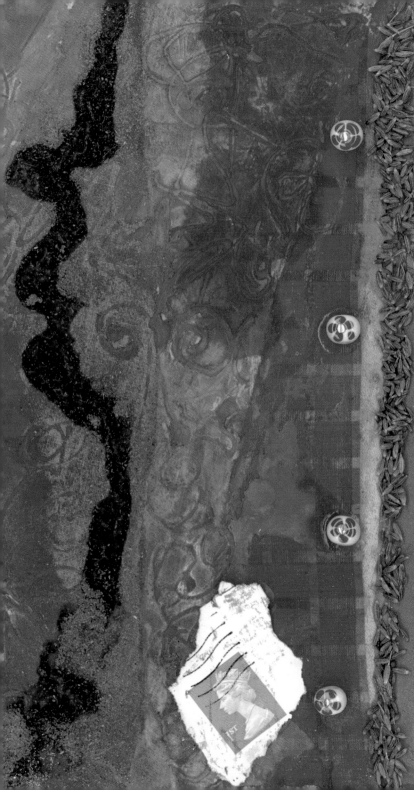

CHICK PEA BURGERS

Squeeze together, an equal amount of cooked **chick peas** and rolled **oats**, 1 handful each per person served. Per person served, add ½ diced **onion** and 1 tsp of **mixed herbs**. **Salt** to taste. Add water until the mix holds together, an **egg** provides extra 'glue' if desired. Shape into burgers, roll in cashews if allergies allow and shallow fry in very little **oil**.

CHICK & POTATO CURRY

For a good sized group, or for freezing in smaller portions, use 4 cups each of cooked **chick peas** and cooked bite size **potatoes.** In a large pan fry a tsp each of grated **garlic** and **ginger** in **sunflower oil**. Add a couple of **onions**, either chopped very finely or liquidised. Cook 5 mins. Add a heaped tsp each of **ground cumin, cumin seeds, ground coriander, dried methi** and **fennel seeds.** Stir, to avoid sticking. After another 5mins mix in 1 Tbl of **tomato purée**, 1 ½ pints of water, the chick peas and potatoes. Add more liquid to prevent catching if required. Simmer for about 20 mins. **Salt** to taste.

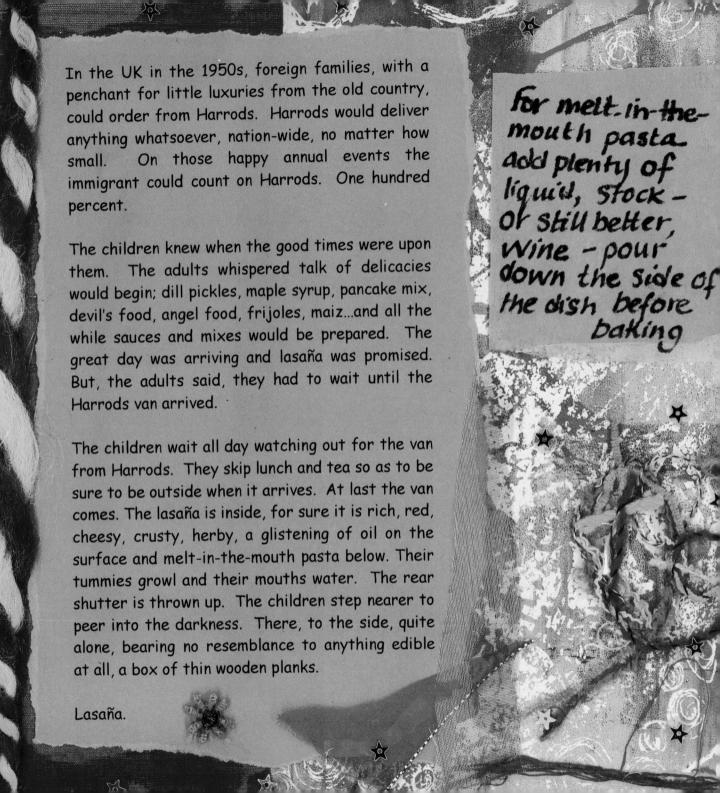

In the UK in the 1950s, foreign families, with a penchant for little luxuries from the old country, could order from Harrods. Harrods would deliver anything whatsoever, nation-wide, no matter how small. On those happy annual events the immigrant could count on Harrods. One hundred percent.

The children knew when the good times were upon them. The adults whispered talk of delicacies would begin; dill pickles, maple syrup, pancake mix, devil's food, angel food, frijoles, maiz...and all the while sauces and mixes would be prepared. The great day was arriving and lasaña was promised. But, the adults said, they had to wait until the Harrods van arrived.

The children wait all day watching out for the van from Harrods. They skip lunch and tea so as to be sure to be outside when it arrives. At last the van comes. The lasaña is inside, for sure it is rich, red, cheesy, crusty, herby, a glistening of oil on the surface and melt-in-the-mouth pasta below. Their tummies growl and their mouths water. The rear shutter is thrown up. The children step nearer to peer into the darkness. There, to the side, quite alone, bearing no resemblance to anything edible at all, a box of thin wooden planks.

Lasaña.

for melt-in-the-mouth pasta add plenty of liquid, stock - or still better, wine - pour down the side of the dish before baking

LASAÑA

This is an oven baked dish of layers, the wide flat pasta called **lasaña** is every other layer between **cottage cheese**, **bechamél sauce** (see YELLOW section), **tomato pasta sauce** (see RED section) and **cheese**. Start with a made or bought tomato pasta sauce for a first layer about 2cm/1" deep into the bottom of a oven proof dish and continue alternating sauces and cheeses with lasaña pasta until the dish is full. Top with cheese and bake slowly, about an hour until the pasta is soft. The work is in making the sauces. The assembly is easy and fast.

SWEETPOTATO MOUSSE

Sweet potatoes cook more quickly than ordinary ones and peel more easily too. Peel and chop 8 orange (not white) **sweet potatoes**, and cook until soft. Drain and whizz with a good handful of **cream cheese**, a chopped **onion**, four **eggs** and a tsp of **salt**. Pour into a greased oven proof dish and bake at medium heat for 40 minutes until set and browning. Serve hot as a main meal, cold as a pâté or dip.

67

FRIJOLES

JAMÓN

LEMON GRASS
SAUCE

SALMÓN

Granada was Europe's last Muslim city and remained so, in total isolation, for 500 years. When Granada finally fell to the Spanish Inquisitors, the local followers of Allah were put to the Catholic sword. It is sometimes said that pork is eaten there so widely so as to demonstrate the local acceptance of the conqueror, by accepting the pigs.

Antonio used to cook pork on every occasion, on the terraza in spring, in his open fire in the winter fuelled by felled olive groves making way for the tourist economy, at the beach in full summer, over charcoal, sprayed with sand. If the light was right, his chin glistening with pork fat, grinning over the embers, discarding the bones, the Moor in him shone through. Doubtless his ancestors would be sorry to know he no longer kept the dietary laws, sorry to see the wine sliding down his throat. But they would surely be proud to know he kept the Islamic laws of generosity and hospitality. A man can always change his diet, it's a lot harder to change his nature.

Put a bag of flour on a roast straight from the oven & let it cool. The weight will make it slice wafer thin

FRIJOLES aka REFRIED BEANS

Pinto beans are best but red kidney beans will do, or even borlotti beans. In desperation boiled black beans can just about pass. Simply soak the beans overnight, cook until soft or, alternatively, open a can. For each cup of beans per person served add ½ an **onion** either fried in **olive oil**, or, for less fat, just added raw to the beans. Whizz up with ¼ tsp **ground cumin** per cup beans, 1 Tbl sieved or fresh **tomatoes** and **salt** to taste. In Mexico the whole mix is smashed and fried in pig fat…

JAMÓN

Use a big fatty ham. Tear off the skin and score the fat in criss-crosses. Stab a clove into every other square and slap on dark brown sugar followed by the juice from a can of peaches or some apple juice. Throw in a cinnamon stick and bake in a medium oven, 20 minutes to the pound, or half kilo, and a further 20 minutes on top heat to brown off the fat. Serve hot or cold.

Kika had a generous heart. She opened her home and her kitchen to anyone interested in food and from there taught a generation of young women how to make the traditional dishes of the village. Occasionally she introduced something new, a slice of apple in the salad. Consternation! But mostly she kept to the traditional recipes, fish in rock salt, potatoes in olive oil, wine in quantity. She also kept to tried and tested methods: buy fresh, buy quality, keep it simple.

immerse smoked fish in a tall jug of

a saucer.

Wait 5 mins.

boiling water + top with

Ready to eat & no smell...

LEMON GRASS SAUCE

A truly delicate sauce for dipping fried foods or dressing salads, this is a wonderful shade of pale coral. Whizz in one cup of **salad oil** a seeded **red chilli**. Dice tiny, tiny, tiny, 3 **spring onions**, 2 stalks of **lemon grass**. Include all the stems. Add 1 tsp grated fresh **ginger**, 1 tsp **sugar**, 1 cup **white wine** or **rice vinegar** (cider is too harsh). **Salt** to taste. Best left overnight. Adjust seasonings to taste.

SALMÓN

Buy a whole fresh gutted **salmon**. Lay on a bed of **coarse sea salt** in a baking tray. If too long, let the head and tail hang over the sides. Cover the rest completely in salt with no part left exposed. Bake in a hot oven until the salt forms a rock hard shell and remains intact even when tapped vigourously, at least 30 mins, more likely 45-50. Remove dish from oven to rest 5 mins. Rake out and discard as much salt as possible. Crack and discard the salt off the top of the fish bringing the skin with it. Invert a plate over the fish and turn it out. Crack the salt and skin off the bottom. Result: a moist, pink, barely salty fish.

aubergine flan
&
cabbage seeds in tamari
olives
&
tofu & cranberry
cheesecake

Simon sent so much cabbage one winter that Lisa referred to it as her cabbage mountain. It was almost as high as the celery mountain from the previous summer when, just as with the cabbage, no-one remembered to change the order and Simon just kept on sending it.

There's a limit to how exciting a dish can be when comprised of cabbage, and cabbage alone. But reaching for seeds, with little volume, and adding rich flavour from a few drops, the mountain was finally moved, looked good, tasted good and was:

cabbage cabbage, the musical fruit,
the more you eat, the more you toot,
the more you toot, the better you feel,
so we'll have cabbage for another meal...'

Use aubergines like little sponges to soak up olive oil, tomato sauces – they then release the flavour in your mouth!

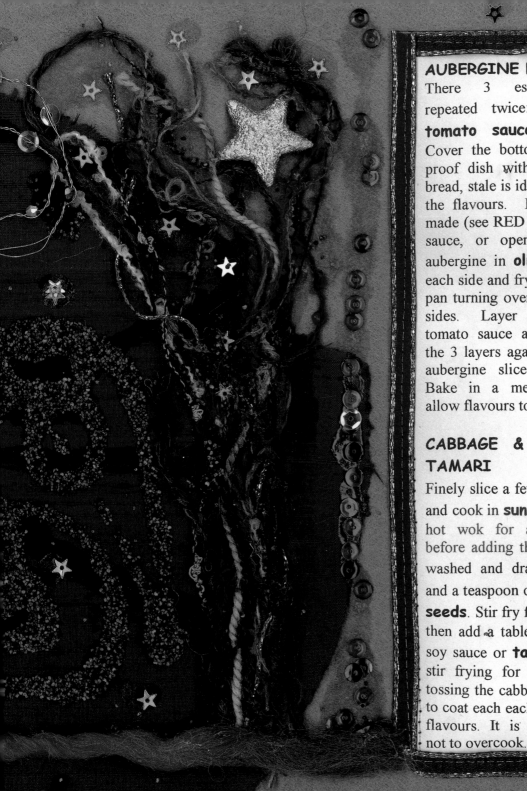

AUBERGINE FLAN

There 3 essential layers repeated twice: **aubergines**, **tomato sauce** and **bread**. Cover the bottom of an oven proof dish with sliced quality bread, stale is ideal as it absorbs the flavours. Layer on home made (see RED section) tomato sauce, or open a jar. Dip aubergine in **olive oil** to coat each side and fry in a dry frying pan turning over to brown both sides. Layer on top of the tomato sauce and then repeat the 3 layers again, ending with aubergine slices on the top. Bake in a medium oven to allow flavours to mingle.

CABBAGE & SEEDS IN TAMARI

Finely slice a few **garlic** cloves and cook in **sunflower oil** in a hot wok for a few seconds before adding the finely sliced, washed and drained **cabbage** and a teaspoon or two of **poppy seeds**. Stir fry for a minute and then add a tablespoon or so of soy sauce or **tamari**. Continue stir frying for a few seconds tossing the cabbage all the time to coat each each shred with the flavours. It is very important not to overcook.

Tofu Ron has a pony tail and a tofu manufacturing company that turns over several tons of soya beans a week. He eats what he makes, sauces sweet and savoury, tofu grilled with shoyu, chunked up in stir-fries, smoked, apple cured, you name it...

He started in the corner of a friend's bakery with a domestic food processor and now churns out most of the UK's solid tofu blocks, supplying his wares nationwide. A common success tale, usually accompanied by stories of how things were in the good old bad old days. Not at all.

Instead, Tofu Ron says, 'do what you do well, what you know you know, and, hey, you don't need everyone to buy your tofu, you just need enough people to buy it to pay your bills...'

Tofu and dairy cheesecakes are interchangeable: substitute tofu & soya milk for eggs, milk and cheese — have some fun...

OLIVES

Purple olives are fairly uncommon outside of Spain but are worth looking out for. Always large like plums, they are called *gordales* and grow principally at lower altitude. Due to their size they are cut before processing to ensure that the flesh is permeated with both brine and the flavour of wild herbs, garlic and citrus. They will keep indefinitely if steeped in **extra virgin oil** and are a superb dish in their own right. They should be served with bread, cheese or salad.

TOFU & CRANBERRY CHEESECAKE

Make a wheat free base with 4 teacups of **oats**, 1 teacup each of melted **margarine** and **sugar** and a pinch of **salt** and press into a pie dish. In a calibrated jug, whizz a block of solid **tofu** (400g), the same quantity of **cranberries**, 1 cup of **sugar**, zest and juice of an **orange**, **soya milk** to take the quantity to 2 ½ pints. As cranberries can be bitter check for sweetness and adjust as necessary. Bake in a slow oven for up to 2 hours until set. Serve cold. Feel free to substitute any berries or soft fruit for cranberries.

CHILI SIN CARNE

RASPBERRY RELISH

gram balls in sweet & sour sauce

RASPBERRY VINEGAR

salsa fresca

SALSA PARA PASTA

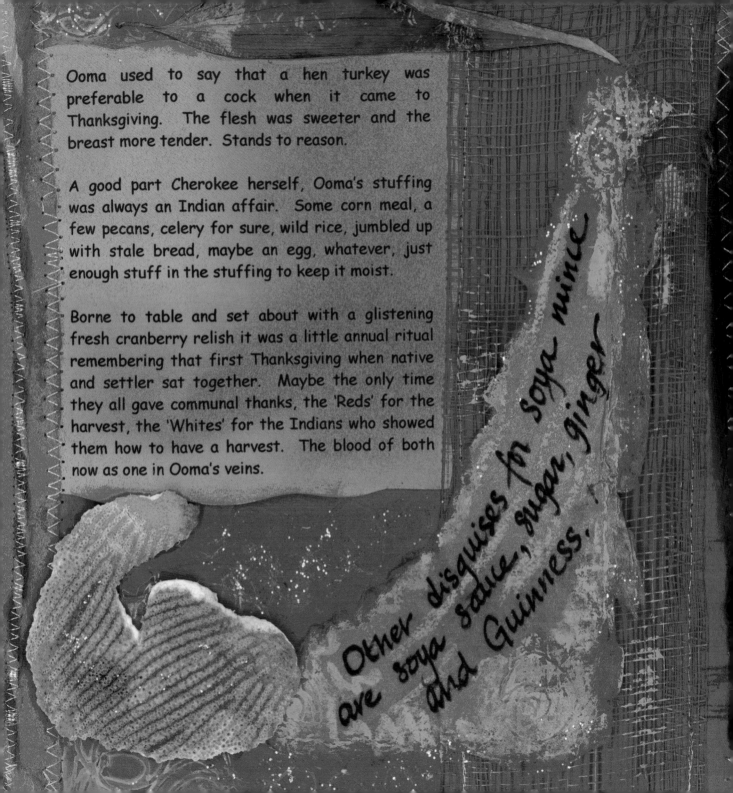

Ooma used to say that a hen turkey was preferable to a cock when it came to Thanksgiving. The flesh was sweeter and the breast more tender. Stands to reason.

A good part Cherokee herself, Ooma's stuffing was always an Indian affair. Some corn meal, a few pecans, celery for sure, wild rice, jumbled up with stale bread, maybe an egg, whatever, just enough stuff in the stuffing to keep it moist.

Borne to table and set about with a glistening fresh cranberry relish it was a little annual ritual remembering that first Thanksgiving when native and settler sat together. Maybe the only time they all gave communal thanks, the 'Reds' for the harvest, the 'Whites' for the Indians who showed them how to have a harvest. The blood of both now as one in Ooma's veins.

Other disguises for soya mince are soya sauce, sugar, ginger and Guinness.

CHILLI SIN CARNE

Using soya mince works well for this dish since soya mince has a somewhat metallic aftertaste and therefore needs a good disguise to be palatable. Dice and sauté a big **onion** in **olive oil**. When it is translucent add two fistsful of **soya mince**. Before it catches either add **red wine** or **sieved tomatoes** or a combination of both to cover the mince entirely plus a Tbl of **tomato purée**. Cook until the mince is soft and not chewy. Add **Tabasco** and **salt** to taste. Finally fold in 4 Tbl cooked **red kidney beans**, two chopped **fresh tomatoes** and either chopped **spring onion** tips, **parsley** or **coriander**.

CRANBERRY RELISH

This is the most outstanding cranberry relish ever. It needs no cooking and is a perfect accompaniment to roasted meats, vegetables, cheeses and pâtés. Pulverise **cranberries** and **fresh oranges** in equal measure. Add **sugar** to taste. That's it…

Gulab jaman are those fat sweet Indian balls that Sakina used to make steeped in syrup. Popped in the mouth as one, they explode with a liquid nectar. Fried well beyond blood heat, they are tossed steaming from the fat into a syrup of rose-water and green cardamoms. As they cool all the flavours are absorbed from the sauce only to be released in the dark privacy of the eater's mouth.

Sakina used this trick of dry fried heated balls and cold sweet sauces well beyond the boundaries of gulab jamans. She tossed deep fried balls of all persuasions into every type of cold sauce with an almost indecent haste. And never lacked for punters...

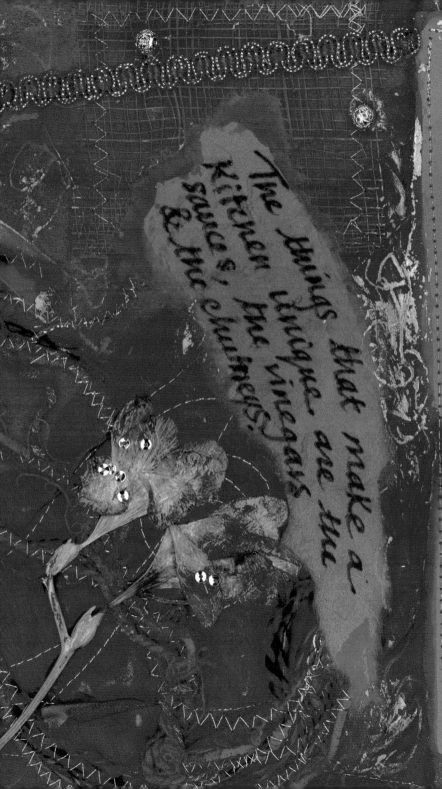

The things that make a kitchen unique are the sauces; the vinegars & the chutneys.

GRAM BALLS IN SWEET AND SOUR SAUCE

Sweet and sour sauce is a simple combination **of tomato purée**, **vinegar** and **sugar** in whatever proportion suits individual taste plus a dash of **soya sauce**. Create a thin sauce by watering down the purée with water and vinegar. Set aside. Create a paste of **gram flour** and water, add chopped **onions** if desired. Drop by spoonsful into hot **oil** and deep fry. When they are golden brown remove them from the fat and drop them into the sauce. The shock of the colder liquid will make them suck in the sauce.

RASPBERRY VINEGAR

Never buy raspberry vinegar, or blackcurrant for that matter, when it is so easy to make at home. Take a good quality **white wine vinegar**, add the fruit, either **raspberries** or **blackcurrants**, and watch it turn red. The colour will begin to change immediately and after a few days the berries will be completely white and the vinegar a wonderful shade of red with an outstanding flavour.

Time was the highway south of San Diego dropped off to dirt at the frontier into Mexico. Everything is different now. These days the border is open and the highway seamless into Tijuana.

Despite the changes, just north in San Juan Capistrano, there is a kaff where the salsa is still extraordinary. Coarse chopped tomatoes are salted enough to make them shed their juice, but not so much as to make the skins wrinkle or the fruit lose its lustre. It's littered with diced spring onions and chopped coriander, but chopped in such a way that the frill of the leaves is somehow intact. How is that? Strive as one might chopping herbs their leaves never emerge with the frill intact...

And then Tabasco, ahh, the king of kings when it comes to chilli sauce. However much the gourmet may sneer at its commonality, who is to say that what is common has no value?

SALSA FRESCA

Dice fresh **tomatoes**, enough to suit the numbers served. Scrape them into a bowl with as much of the juice as possible. Chop **onions** finely, spring, red or white. The onions should be a 1/4 of the quantity of tomatoes. Add. Chop the same amount of **fresh coriander** as onions. Add. Then **salt** and **Tabasco** to taste. The salt will sweat the tomatoes, the juice is as good as the salsa.

SALSA PARA PASTA

Fry **onions** in **olive oil** (1 onion between 2 people). Add chopped **peppers**, any colour or all colours (1 between 2 people). When the vegetables are browning the water has cooked off. Now fry **tomato purée**, twice the quantity as the vegetables. Add four times the quantity of diced **tomatoes**, **salt** and a small teaspoon of **sugar**. Remove from heat and finally add chopped fresh herbs of your choice, **basil**, **oregano**, **marjoram**. Serve over **pasta**.

Mediterranean taste: first steps, create a base of onions, peppers and tomatoes fried in olive oil — heavy on the salt—

BURRITOS

CHIMICHANGAS

CREMA CATALANA

FRENCH ONION TART

HUMOUS

MOUSSAKA

POTATO SALADS

RAITA

STRING HOPPERS

TOFU KEBABS

Burrito in English means 'little ass'. Robert always declared he spoke no Spanish. Yet he silently reckoned up his grocery bill in Spanish until the day he died. Perhaps he didn't know that a native language almost always shines through when it comes to prayer or mental arithmetic. For in Robert this was probably the last vestige of a 1920s schooling where the children all strove to pass as 'whites' because the Indians and Hispanics only counted as half a child when it came to getting government funds. And who wanted half a pencil or half a book when there were whole ones around? When he was sixty he was suddenly single and he took to cooking for himself like a cat to water. Until that is, he came across chimichangas. He used the parcels, like their donkey namesake to carry things: at first the traditional burrito fillings, then moved on to chicken, cheese, duck and plum sauce, grated tofu with miso and onions, finally apples, sugar and cinnamon, topped with cream. A non-stop feast of tortilla wrapped surprises were fed constantly to his friends, many of whom were unhappy with the influx of Mexican labour in the Salinas Valley. Robert referred mischievously to his friends as his 'burrito' buddies. Surely he meant they ate burritos...

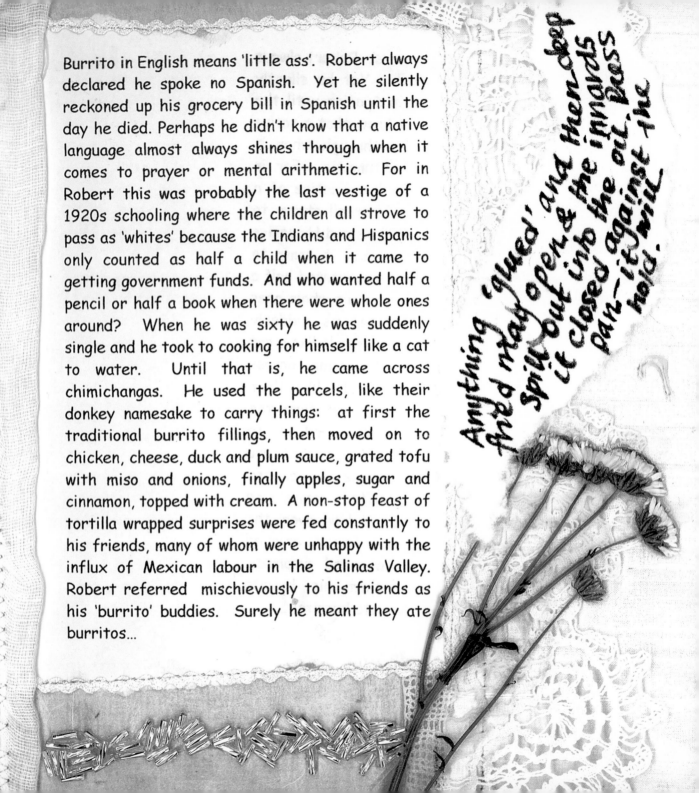

Anything 'glued' and then deep fried may open & the innards spill out into the oil. Press it closed against the pan — it will hold.

BURRITOS

Any **flour tortilla** will act as the wrapper for burritos which vary in content from city to city, street to street. Wrap the tortilla around **refried beans** (in variations in the PINK section) they are easy to make: smash up by hand, or with a liquidiser, 1 Tbl cooked **pinto beans** per burrito, (red kidney will do), with diced raw **onion**, tsp of **ground cumin**, **salt**, tsp **tomato pureé**. Top with fresh tomato **salsa** (in the RED section…), **jalepeño chillies**, **lettuce** and **cheese** (optional). If the beans were cold, the whole package should be warmed.

CHIMICHANGAS

Exactly the same as burritos but deep fried. Therefore they need 'glue'. **Flour** and **water** is the glue. Glue along the final seam and let them rest. Deep fry in **sunflower oil**.

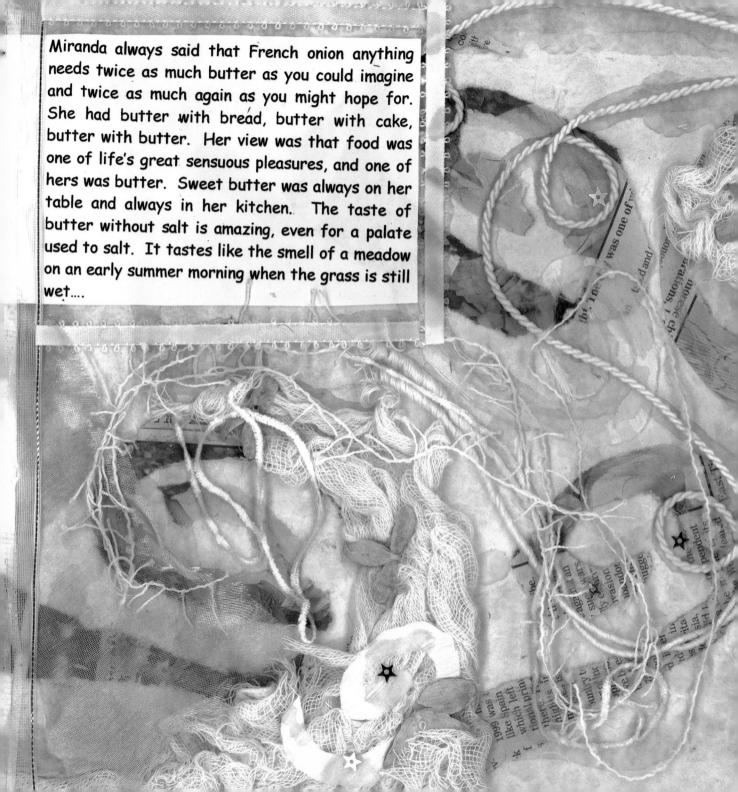

Miranda always said that French onion anything needs twice as much butter as you could imagine and twice as much again as you might hope for. She had butter with bread, butter with cake, butter with butter. Her view was that food was one of life's great sensuous pleasures, and one of hers was butter. Sweet butter was always on her table and always in her kitchen. The taste of butter without salt is amazing, even for a palate used to salt. It tastes like the smell of a meadow on an early summer morning when the grass is still wet....

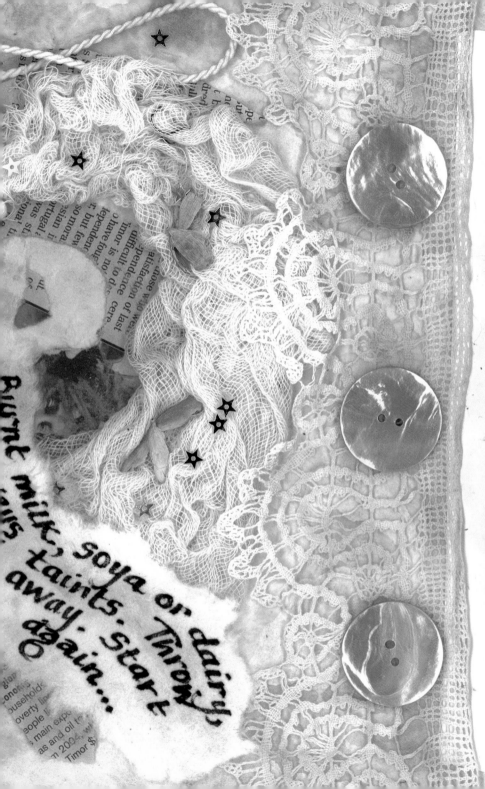

Burnt milk, soya or dairy, taints. Throw it away. Start again...

CREMA CATALANA

A bit like crème brulée but without the crème or the brulée. A bit like an exotic rice pudding but without the rice or the pudding. In other words this version defies description. In a litre of **soya milk** cook half a teacup of **rice flour**, an equal amount of **brown sugar** and 5 **cardamom** pods. Don't even think about leaving out the cardamoms! Ideally crack them open. When thickened remove from heat, add a tsp of **vanilla**, some **orange zest** and a squeeze of **lemon**. Remember a pinch of **salt**. The longer left the more the flavours infuse. Serve warm or cold, grilled with brown sugar or topped with sweet creams (FAWN).

FRENCH ONION TART

Rich in butter, this is a variation on quiche (YELLOW), where half the milk is replaced by **cream cheese**. For 1 quiche use ½ pack (250g) of **sweet butter** and at least 4 **onions**. Cook down until the onions are soft, break up, are brown and scarcely resemble onions at all. Add a scant tsp of **brown sugar** and a pinch of

93

Matt's patience was already tested by his lodger's noisy 2am cooking sprees. After just such a restless night, on entering the kitchen Matt surfed the entire length of the kitchen atop a half eaten fried egg that she had dropped on the floor, and finally came to a stop by falling over. On the verge of eviction (or murder) the errant cook saved the day with a dish of houmous. Specially prepared to titillate taste buds, it was framed above him in her hands. Little did Matt know the ingredients of the peace offering were purloined from his own cupboards.

Open tins of tomatoes using the left hand anti-clockwise — it makes the tomatoes taste sweeter.
(only joking...)

HOUMOUS

Liquidise or mash together 2 cups of cooked **chick peas**, 1 tsp grated **garlic**, 1 tsp **salt**, 1 Tbl **tahini** (sesame paste), the juice of 1 **lemon** and ½ cup of water. Texture can be varied according to how little or much it is mashed. Add more or less water depending on whether a pâté or a dip is required. Stir in fresh chopped **parsley**.

MOUSSAKA

Gluten free, this makes a great alternative to lasaña or aubergine bake. To make sufficient for 6 healthy appetites choose a deep oven proof pan about the size of a telephone directory. Layer sliced, cooked, drained **potatoes** alternatively with tinned or home-made **tomato sauce** (in the RED section...) and with sliced, olive oil sauteéed **aubergines**. Use more or less of each depending on the season and the price of aubergines. Try and ensure that there are at least two layers of each. Top with either a vegan or dairy **white sauce** (see YELLOW section...), or a gluten free mix of **egg** and **yoghurt**. Bake for 45 minutes in a medium oven.

There is a story about Sherman who worked in the post room of a large San Francisco office block which can't be told here. It concerns his considerable personal prowess. For he was as famous for it as he was his contribution of potato salad to the annual summer picnic organised by the company, (where incidentally he also contributed his unmentionable quality to select revellers). Speaking only of his salad, it was generous, not just a load of potatoes with a few interesting diversions, but every mouthful a combination of textures, the crunchy with the soft, the gritty with the smooth. Salt and sharp and deeply satisfying. Sometimes, just to surprise everyone, he was heavy with the mustard, and the salad moved from the sea of white with the little coloured pieces bobbing below the surface clothing of mayo, to a more brilliant sunshine coating with the white of the egg pushing through. It would be interesting to know if Sherman would be pleased to be remembered for his salad rather than something else.

POTATO SALAD

Peel (or not) one big **potato** for each person served. Cut into bite sized pieces and boil until soft. Drain and cool. Add ½ hard-boiled **egg** per person. To this whole volume add half the volume each of: chopped **celery**, diced **spring onions** or **red onions**, red, yellow and orange **peppers**, green or black **olives**, baby or diced **gherkins**, chopped **cucumber**. Add **salt** and chopped fresh **mint** to taste. Dress with **mayonnaise** and a dash of mustard and vinegar. For vegan salad, delete the eggs and the mayo and dress with **mustard seeds** emulsified (fancy word for seriously ground up in oil) in **olive oil** with **vinegar** and **coarse black pepper**.

RAITA

A sauce for any piquant food, blend plain **yoghurt** with fresh **mint**, **cucumber** and **sugar**, thinned with **milk** or water. For vegan version, use **tofu**.

boil the eggs in with the potatoes

Save time & energy!

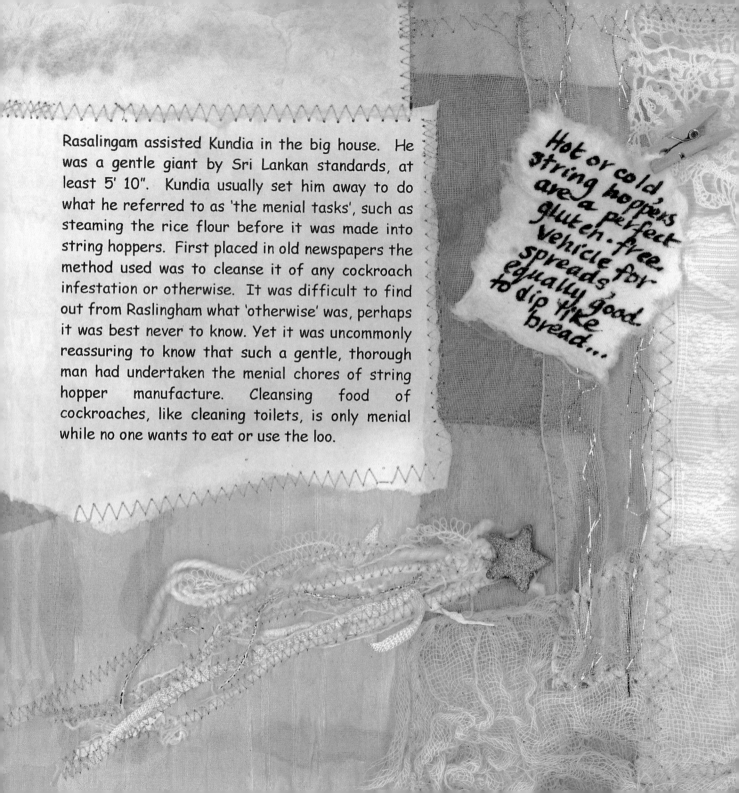

Rasalingam assisted Kundia in the big house. He was a gentle giant by Sri Lankan standards, at least 5' 10". Kundia usually set him away to do what he referred to as 'the menial tasks', such as steaming the rice flour before it was made into string hoppers. First placed in old newspapers the method used was to cleanse it of any cockroach infestation or otherwise. It was difficult to find out from Raslingham what 'otherwise' was, perhaps it was best never to know. Yet it was uncommonly reassuring to know that such a gentle, thorough man had undertaken the menial chores of string hopper manufacture. Cleansing food of cockroaches, like cleaning toilets, is only menial while no one wants to eat or use the loo.

Hot or cold, string hoppers are a perfect gluten-free vehicle for spreads, equally good to dip like bread...

STRING HOPPERS

The string hopper originates in Sri Lanka and is a traditional accompaniment to curries. Mix a good two handfuls of **rice flour** with **water** to a paste stiff enough to hold itself into a sphere. Pinch off portions large enough to fit in the hopper of a potato ricer and then squeeze them through. Out they come like spaghetti in long white strings. Practise a few times returning the paste to the hopper. Then, straight into the steamer, swirl the strings as they exit the ricer by moving the ricer in a circle. This will make little patties in the steamer like worm casts. Try not to pile them into little hills, they are better as flat as possible. Steam them over water for 3-5 mintues. Cool, peel off the steamer bottom and they are string hoppers.

TOFU KEBABS

Use the hard **tofu**, not the soft stuff, and cut into cubes. Thread with any chunky **vegetables** onto a skewer. Shallow fry in an oiled pan at top heat, turning the skewers constantly. As the tofu browns and the vegetables cook, in the final moments throw on **soya sauce** or **tamari**, which is gluten-free, to sizzling savoury affect…

99

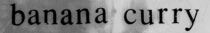

banana curry

BANANA PONE

BROCCOLLI BAKE

citrus cheesecake

curried cheeseball

EGGS HALDI

QUICHE

spanish omlette

Orangutans were the subject of a fund-raising effort in York one year. Food was a contribution being sought. What would be portable? What would be tempting? But perhaps the most important question, what would the orangutans like if they were invited?

When the vast paella pans are cranked up in the streets of The Quarter, York on high days and holidays, strangers flock to taste the salt sweet savoury. Even the sceptical cannot resist the smell and sight of the topaz curry, bananas and coconut thickly contrasted with brilliant green coriander leaves and bedded in a tortilla wrap. All thanks to the orangutan in everyone...

Eastern taste: first steps, create a base of the holy trinity, that is, garlic, ginger and onions fried in bland oils, (ie veg., soya etc), easy on the salt, then add the rest...

BANANA CURRY

In 2 Tbl **sunflower** or **soya oil** fry the 'holy trinity', in other words, **garlic, onions** and **ginger**. For this recipe, a teaspoon of each, finely chopped or grated. When they are translucent, but ideally not <u>not</u> brown, add a teaspoon of **madras curry powder** followed quickly by six peeled and sliced **bananas**. Don't be fooled: bananas take longer to peel and slice than you think…Fry all lightly and restrain from over-stirring or the fruit will break up. Within only a few minutes add **coconut milk** to just cover the fruit, bring to the boil, add **salt**. Remove from the heat. Stir in chopped **fresh coriander**. Eat.

Sitting in a Kansas City church's dark corner waiting for her father, the little girl saw the cleaner. He was a tall, thin, bent out of shape old man. He stopped dusting when he came to the piano and sat down to play. He played a magic ragtime, blues and rockabilly, keeping time by swaying his distorted bony frame. The child crept nearer before he saw her and made him jump. He stopped, and the notes seemed almost to arrest in mid air and then tinkle to the floor.

"Whachew doin' here? Why, you scared the grittin' pone out o' me."

"What's grittin' pone?"

He laughed, a few yellow teeth in an otherwise toothless smile.

"Why chile, pone is what we folks growd up on. Git yer mother to beatcha up some corn meal with eggs, milk and chitlin' fat. Bake you a pone so I kin scare it out o' yew..."

In adult years she made her own version of his pone for breakfast and brunch, against the remembered sounds of ragtime, blues and rockabilly. And the "grittin'" part? Well corn meal is sandy but it makes a good substitute for wheat flour, and, as a rule, is very good for bones and teeth. Although the pianist may have been the exception...

Don't overcook greens, they will look
& taste like used dishcloths. —
Steam-fry is a good fast lick
and it makes the green
greener...

BANANA PONE - *corncake*

Smash together six **bananas**, and a 500g tub of melted **margarine**. Using the tub as a measure, add 1 tub each of **sugar** and **soya milk** and 2 of **corn meal**. Add a tsp each of **baking powder** and **vanilla**, and a pinch of **salt**. In a greased and floured domestic oven-sized roasting dish, bake the batter until a knife comes out clean from the centre.

BROCCOLI BAKE

Steam-fry a head of **broccoli** in hot **olive oil** with a dash or two of water. Set aside in an oven proof dish with a couple of chopped fresh **tomatoes**. Make a pint of béchamel sauce by sauté-ing a teaspoon of **mustard seeds** in 3 Tbl **margarine** or **butter**, remove from heat and stir in 3 Tbl plain **flour**, white or brown, so that every grain is coated in fat. Return to heat and slowly add a pint of **milk**, dairy or soya stirring constantly. 'Slowly add...stirring constantly' is key to avoid lumps. Add a pinch of **salt**; **cheese** if desired. Keep stirring until it thickens. Hey presto, béchamel sauce! Pour over the broccoli and tomatoes, top with cheese and/or **crisps**. Medium bake until browning.

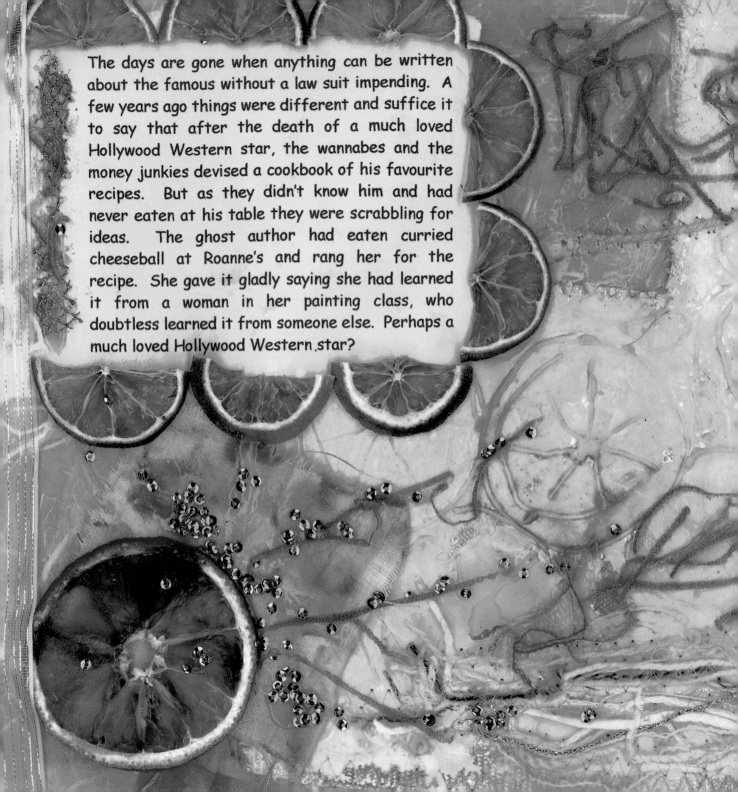

The days are gone when anything can be written about the famous without a law suit impending. A few years ago things were different and suffice it to say that after the death of a much loved Hollywood Western star, the wannabes and the money junkies devised a cookbook of his favourite recipes. But as they didn't know him and had never eaten at his table they were scrabbling for ideas. The ghost author had eaten curried cheeseball at Roanne's and rang her for the recipe. She gave it gladly saying she had learned it from a woman in her painting class, who doubtless learned it from someone else. Perhaps a much loved Hollywood Western star?

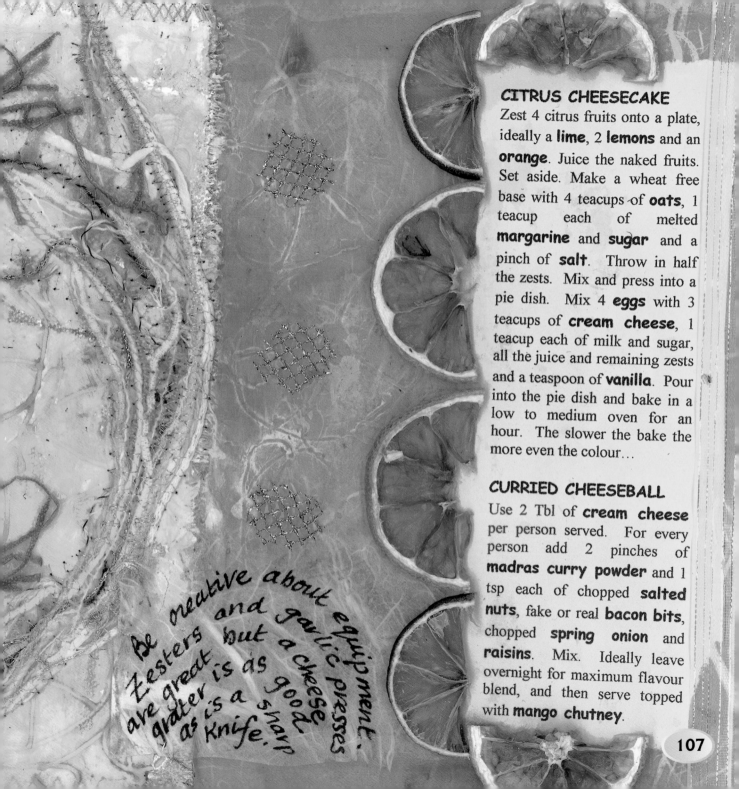

CITRUS CHEESECAKE

Zest 4 citrus fruits onto a plate, ideally a **lime**, 2 **lemons** and an **orange**. Juice the naked fruits. Set aside. Make a wheat free base with 4 teacups of **oats**, 1 teacup each of melted **margarine** and **sugar** and a pinch of **salt**. Throw in half the zests. Mix and press into a pie dish. Mix 4 **eggs** with 3 teacups of **cream cheese**, 1 teacup each of milk and sugar, all the juice and remaining zests and a teaspoon of **vanilla**. Pour into the pie dish and bake in a low to medium oven for an hour. The slower the bake the more even the colour…

CURRIED CHEESEBALL

Use 2 Tbl of **cream cheese** per person served. For every person add 2 pinches of **madras curry powder** and 1 tsp each of chopped **salted nuts**, fake or real **bacon bits**, chopped **spring onion** and **raisins**. Mix. Ideally leave overnight for maximum flavour blend, and then serve topped with **mango chutney**.

Be creative about equipment. Zesters and garlic presses are great but a cheese grater is as good as is a sharp knife.

Sri Lankan tea estate owners call the rows of houses that they have built for their workers 'lines'. On grey concrete floors and within bare walls these people still live and die. Kundia's wife picked tea when she wasn't tending her flowers against the 'lines', but he was released from the drying sheds because he was the cook in the big house.

Coconut milk was Kundia's first lesson in curry making, squeezing the hot water through the dried meat of the coconut twice with his small wizened hands, the first milk for thickening, the second for flavour.

Haldi has a brilliance against the green of spring onions and the white of the eggs. It is as dazzling as blooms against concrete. Through his food, Kundia, now so long dead, still shouts a defiant visual vibrancy in the world.

BASIL & MUSHROOM

Eggs are glue — Add to any sloppy mix, bake and it will set...

fennel & pepper

OREGANO & TOMATO

sauces &

onion ...

EGGS HALDI

Hard boil **eggs**, 1 per person. Halve. Pour over a sauce made with chopped **spring onion** fried lightly in **oil** (not olive!). Use 1 onion for every 2 eggs. When the onion is barely cooked remove from the heat and add a teaspoon of **haldi** (turmeric) for every 4 eggs. Return to the heat, DON'T burn the turmeric but gently fry it. Then add **coconut milk**, 'first milk' only. It will thicken rapidly. Remove and add **salt** to taste. Toss chopped green onion tails on top for colour.

QUICHE

Forget making pastry, it takes too long. Line the pie dish with **tortilla wraps**. The standard mix for an average pie dish is 4 **eggs** beaten with **milk** up to the 1 pint measure and poured over **a chosen filling**. If the choice is 'wet' like tomatoes or mushrooms fry off the liquid a bit first or the result will be sloppy. A handful of grated **cheese**, few **herbs** and a pinch of **salt** complete it. Bake in a medium oven for up to an hour. It's done when it's solid

Such is his pride in his country's cuisine Javier will invite almost any stranger into his Andalusian home to learn how to make tortilla, or Spanish omlette. In one way tortilla is portable scrambled eggs. In another, this thick pancake of eggs, potatoes, olive oil and salt is majestic for its flavour.

In his modest kitchen scarcely equipped by northern European standards Javier says that the potato must be cut is a certain way with primitive razor devices and the onions sliced by hand. He says peeling potatoes is essential, olive oil in lakes is a must for frying and onions are definitely not optional. He also says there is no other way to make tortilla but this one way...

In a sparse kitchen the few utensils, the naked pot sink, the basic ingredients, the bare light bulb, a sort of poverty is suggested. Then the moment comes to reach for the pan. The walk-in cupboard is opened. Within there must be more than eighty frying pans. Isn't it tremendous how priority can be given to passions whatever the circumstances?

Once mastered, use tortilla as a vehicle for other ingredients: peppers, broad beans, leftovers ... even make it vegan by smashing up the potatoes and using them to keep the shape

TORTILLA ESPAÑOLA

Peel, (or not) 4 average **potatoes** and slice them the same size so they cook at the same speed. Add a large sliced **onion**. In a non-stick frying pan fry them deeply in **olive oil** until cooked through. Nothing but olive oil will do and don't be stingy. Remove, draining off the oil, saving it for other culinary events. Gently mix in a tsp **salt** and enough **eggs** to cover the potatoes and then some. Don't be too vigorous or the potatoes will break up. Return the pan to the heat, add a spoonful of oil and pour the mix in. Let it cook on half heat until the edges come away clean. The middle should be drying out before attempting to turn it. Wet a smooth plate that is bigger than the pan. Invert the wet plate over the pan like a lid. In one confident move turn the pan over so that the tortilla is on the plate. Confidence is more important than speed…Slide the tortilla from the wet plate into the pan, give it a push if necessary. Let it continue to cook until the tortilla is solid. Tortilla is very forgiving, even if dropped, broken or ballsed up it can usually be smashed together and made to look presentable, and it always tastes wonderful whatever…

111

EL PIANO

En 1998, en un pueblo pequeño y de poca importancia en el norte de Europa, un restorán abría sus puertas para vender comida vegeteriana en el más cállido ambiente de hospitalidad hispánica, donde se permite fumar y donde todos están invitados a traer su propio vino. Nos gustan la música y el baile. Los niños son siempre bienvenidos. La cocina está a la vista del público; las palabrotas y los chistes así como el estrés y el humor con que se sirve el público están en vidriera constantemente.

La comida es simple. Los pasos son pocos. Todo se prepara en pequeñas cantidades. Por lo tanto, nada dura mucho tiempo y todo es fresco. De vez en cuando, en una cocina separada, se prepara carne y pescado, también de alta calidad, para fiestas privadas en la Sala Rayo de Sol, en la Sala Marroquí la Tercera Sala.

Entre la clientela habitual de El Piano, se pueden encontrar tanto vecinos de la zona como visitantes del mundo entero. El Piano mantiene excelentes relaciones con sus proveedores, ya sean de York o del sur de España. La comida preparada refleja el esfuerzo de toda esa gente que ofrece a la cocina de El Piano lo mejor.
Todas las recetas de este libro vienen de El Piano, en York, donde un equipo comprometido las elabora y las sirve.
Gran parte de nuestro personal también sigue carreras de artistas, esritores, músicos, joyeros,

actores, y universitarios. El Piano se beneficia enormemente del aporte que la experiencia de esta gente da a nuestra empresa, y al mismo tiempo, les da un sostén económico que les permite seguir progresando. Y así, al ritmo del cuchillo cuando se cortan las verduras o de los platos en el agua, se van completando las piezas de los diferentes rompecabezas de las personalidades de El Piano.

Trabajamos en un negocio cuyo motor es la gente que lo forma, y como muestra de nuestro trabajo les

In 1998 a one-horse restaurant in a small provincial town in Northern Europe opened its doors selling vegetarian meals in an atmosphere of Hispanic hospitality. Smoking is permitted everywhere. Diners are invited to bring their own alcohol. Music and dance is encouraged. Children are welcome at any time. The kitchen is open to public view, the swearing and the jokes, the stresses and the humour of serving the public are on full display.

The food is simple. The steps to completion are few. Everything is prepared in small quantities so nothing lasts long and everything is fresh. From time to time in a separate kitchen meat and fish, again simple, again of excellent quality, are prepared for private parties in the Sunshine Room, the Moroccan Room or the Third Room.

El Piano counts among its regular customers local residents as well as visitors from all over the world. It has enviable excellent relations with its suppliers, be they from York or Southern Spain. The food prepared reflects the efforts of all these people to provide the El Piano kitchen with the best.

The recipes in this book are all made at El Piano in York, all the time, and served by a committed crew. Many staff follow parallel careers as artists, writers, musicians, jewellers, performers, carvers, and academics. El Piano benefits hugely from their input to the company through their wide experience.

At the same time El Piano provides an economic platform for them to develop their careers. Against the even rhythm of chopping vegetables or washing pots, people's internal puzzles can often be resolved.

We work in a business which is powered by a social engine and with this book present some aspects of our work with pride.

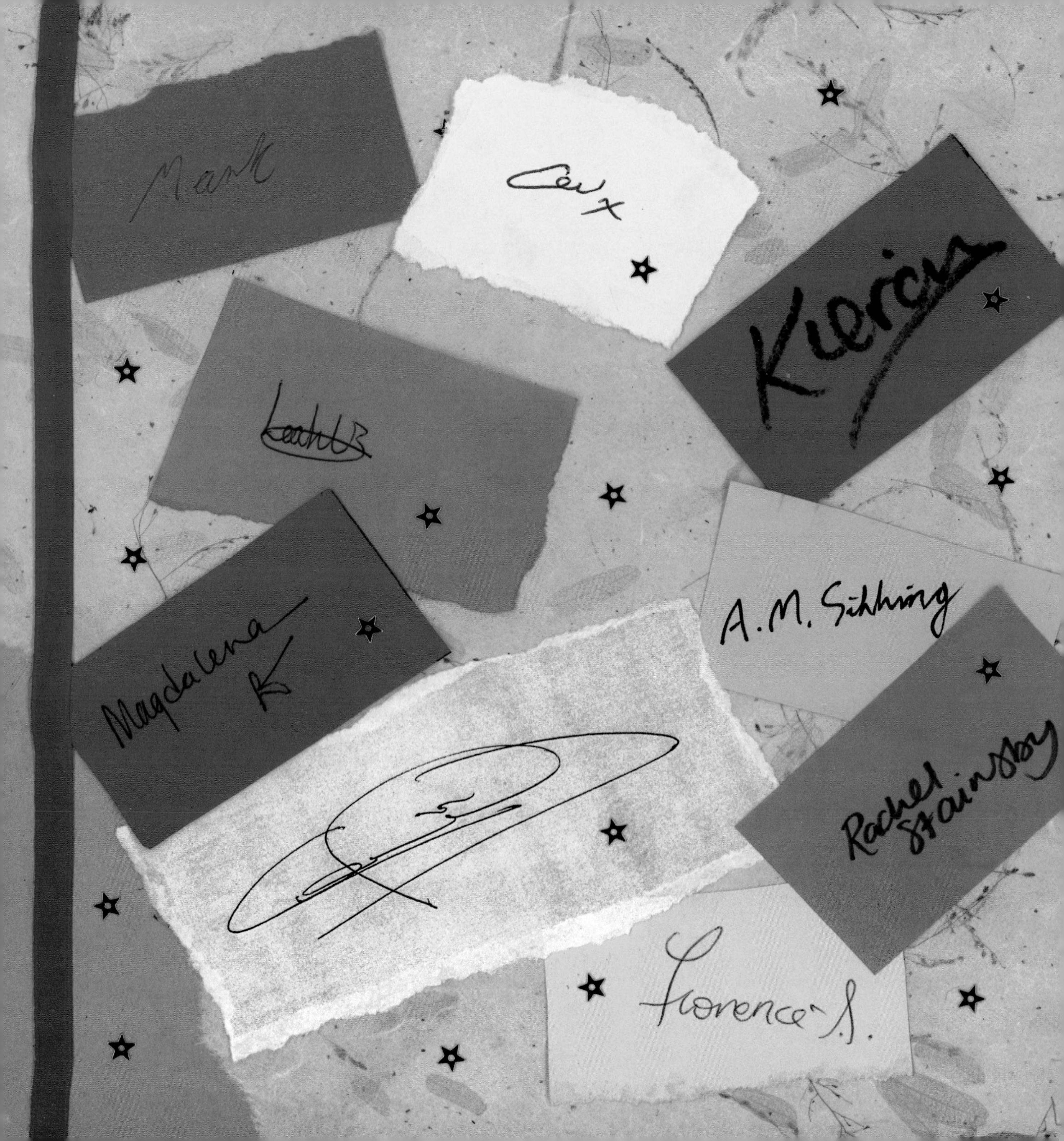
Mark
Kieran
Magdalena
florence S.

Irene Burguest

ASTRID WENDELSTIGH

50 730064
Jelly Belly XX

Bob /X.

Colin E~

Laura
xxx

Cheska

A Ammis(?)

sally

Caroline

Lisa Raman

Coming soon from ENDpapers...

Festival of Angels - a literary thriller

ISBN 0-9543247-1-4

Angeltime

The City of York has a heart but almost no lungs. Its green spaces are diminished, ragged at the edges, made smaller still in winter by rising water, for every year the River Ouse marks itself higher and higher on the flood defences. Ground water seeps, more sewage than sweet. The air is dense with the odour of sugar and chocolate. It hardly moves. Under this layer of aromatic confection is the armature of air, its base molecules, the structure upon which breath rides. If it were solid it would be rock hard. Fossilised. Except for the Minster, or the 'Cathedral' as visitors wrongly call it, where the wind is outrageously behaved, the air in York is still. The plain keeps it tucked in, re-cycling, the same air now as was there two millennia ago. All that ever breathed it, sang with its lift, laughed through its intake, exhaled with its power, sighed in its mercy, are joined. Through the air they share the common needle of living.

Realtime

A stone's throw from the Minster, is The Quarter...a distorted little swastika of narrow streets, home of the annual Festival of Angels. On the evening of this December's ice display Carmen Romero finds Phil Blackmore in The Star and asks;

"What if I told you that a series of events made the police look all bent out of shape and the drugs squad to be, if not corrupt, then stupid?"

"Now wait just a minute..."

"And suppose I could prove that there was a conspiracy between the council, the police, one licensee and his barman to proceed in a business of some considerable importance to all of them. Just suppose I could."

"I'm listening."

"Well, what if I told the tale backwards. What if I said to you a nasty little man decided to move on from small time pimping to dealing drugs. Not soft drugs, the sort you drug squad guys are no longer really interested in, but the sexy stuff, cocaine for example, even smack."

"I'm still listening... "

Festival of Angels *three days, three people, three cultures, one story...*

Coming soon from ENDpapers...

The Alhambra Arcana - a literary thriller

ISBN 0-9543247-2-2

Prologue

...She reached in. The warmest and the darkest place on earth. She couldn't hear the woman's cries, because to have done so would have made her draw back. She simply tuned out everything but her senses of feel and judgement. These were the moments when she knew she didn't believe in God, whatever she might say in polite conversation. Not the God of her fathers anyway, because in these hours of need, it was never that God that she called upon. She called upon memory, her own and those of the other women who had helped her, Ana in Bolivia, Maria Jose in Mexico, and in turn she guessed on all their memories, the God of her mothers. Could she catch this one whole? Silently she breathed "Help her. Help her."

Then after the prayer went up there was always a stillness of quiet purpose which overcame her. It was working on her now. Sliding her hand in, with no room to spare, she met the shoulder, the head well away. She never had any doubt, but if others did, they could not deny it now. The way was hard, and she punctured the sack with her fingers. The waters flooded out onto the bare earth, thick, murky and flowing over the pebbles with a putrefying stench. The child was rotten. She had to be quick. The passage would close and she would only have the unmoving arm. She began to pull on it. She never thought to look up, and later when she remembered every moment, she realised it was just as well. Their horror would have made her falter. Yet in some ways everything was made easier. For when the child is dead, there is only the mother to save, in whatever way you can...

The Alhambra Arcana *a day, a hundred thousand people, a past that lives on...*

LEMONGRASS.
£1.20 BUNCH
PRODUCE OF THAILAND